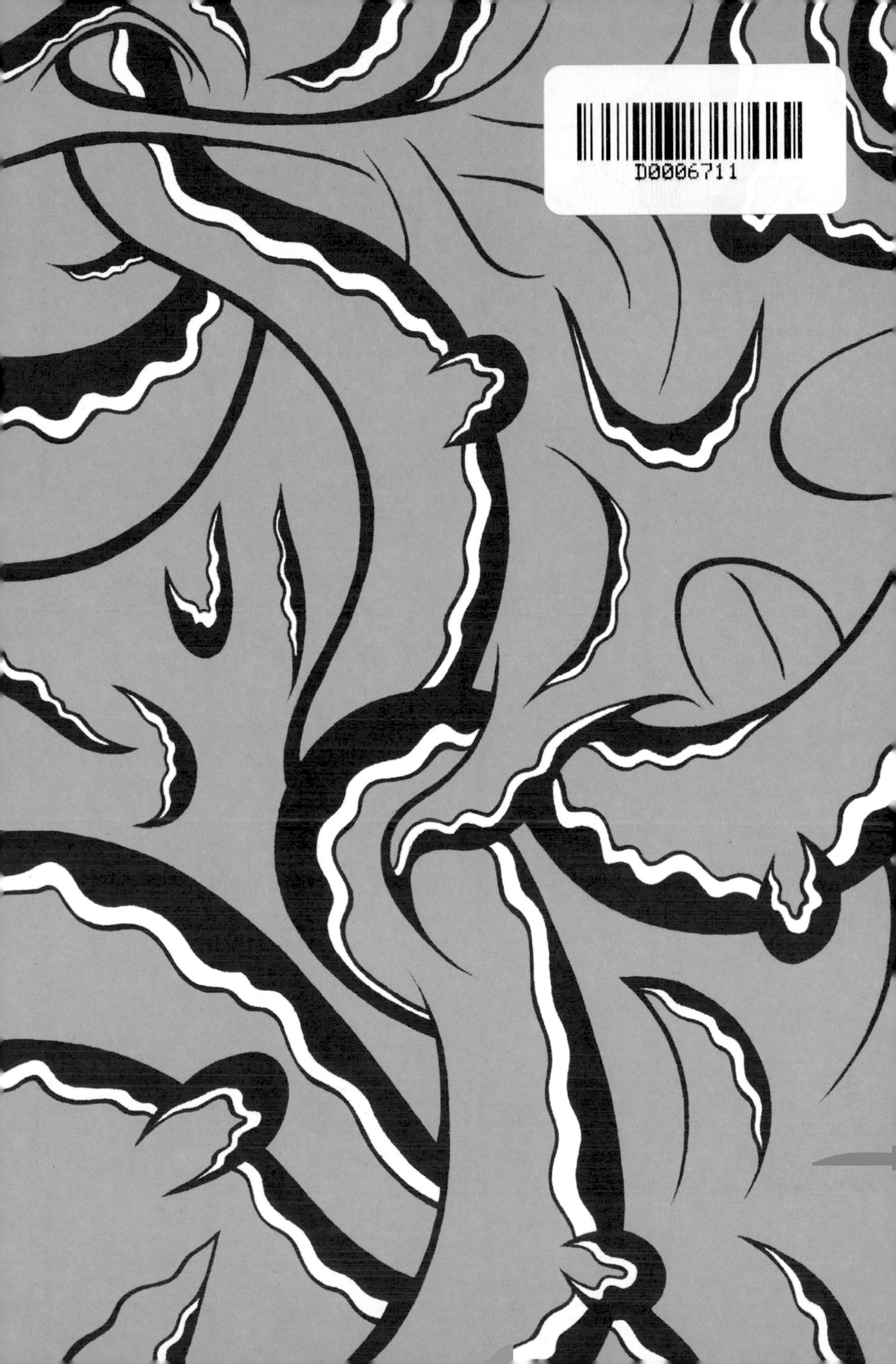

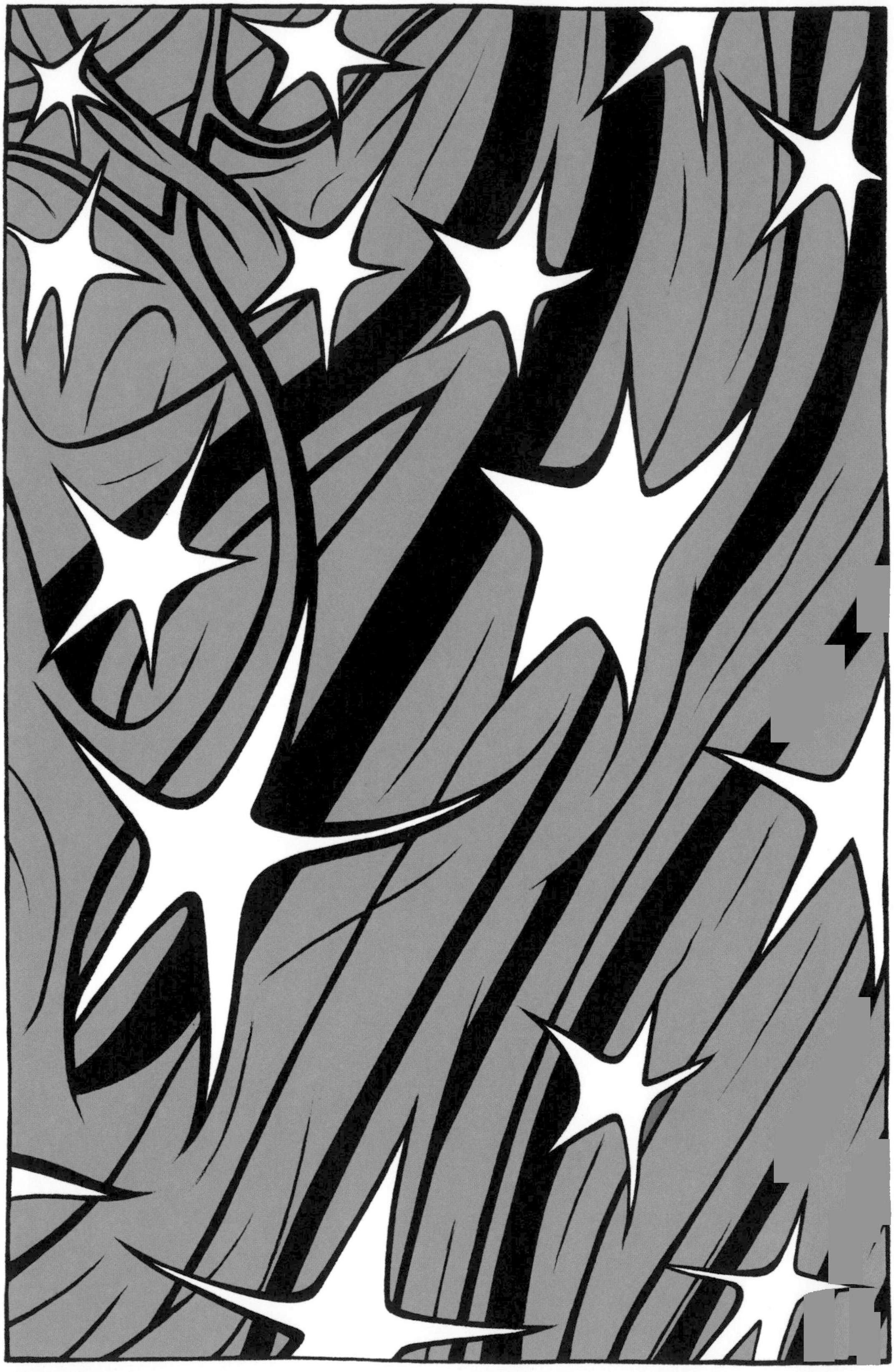

CRYPTOID

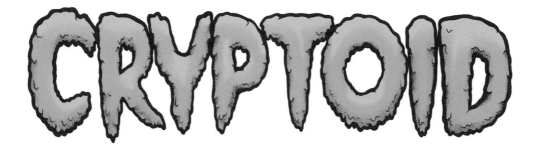

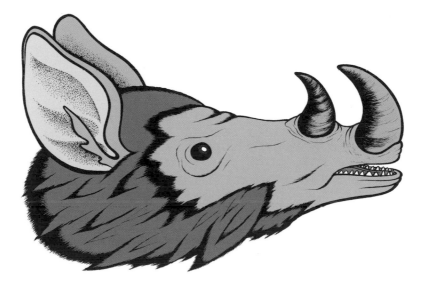

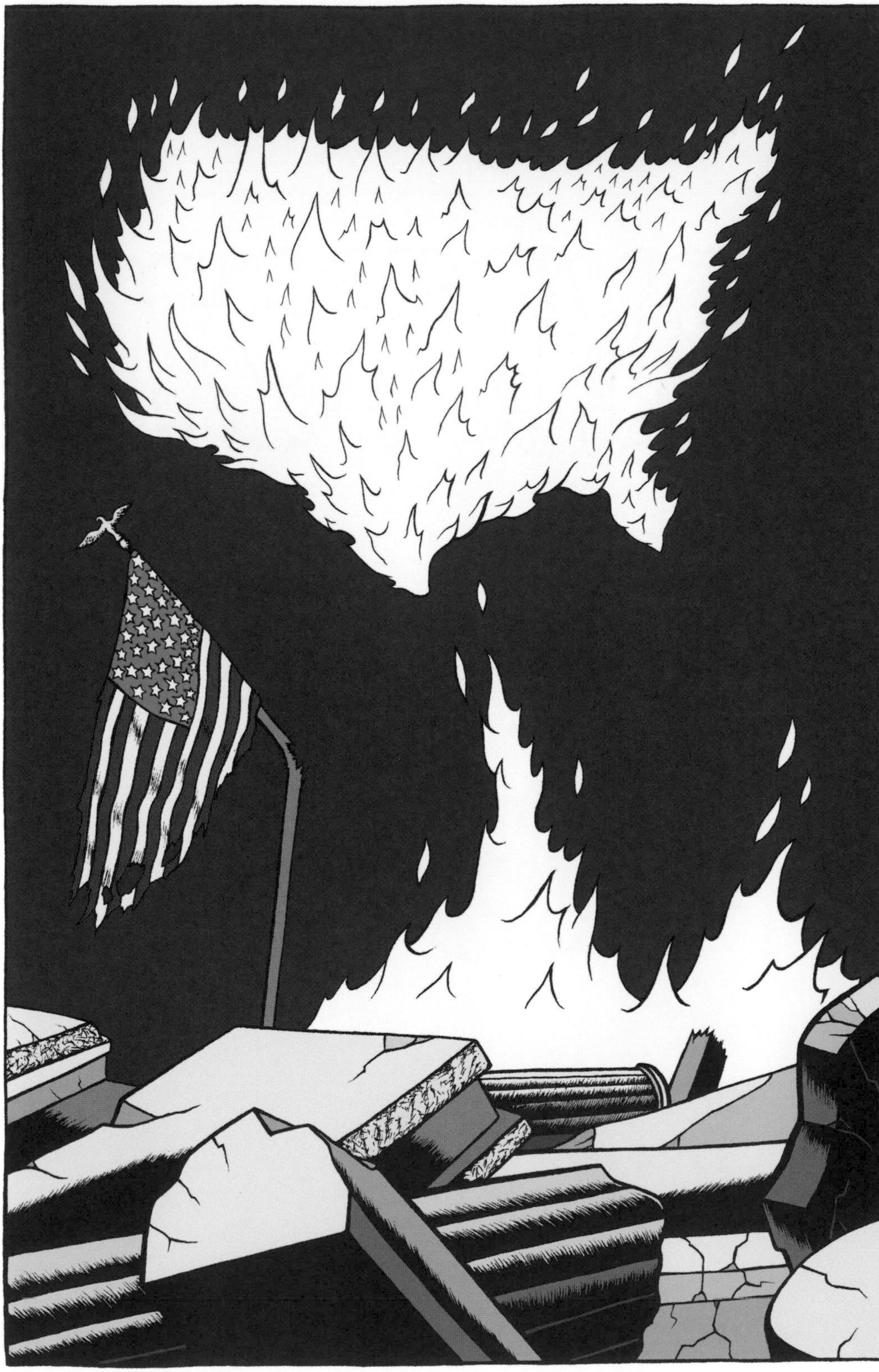

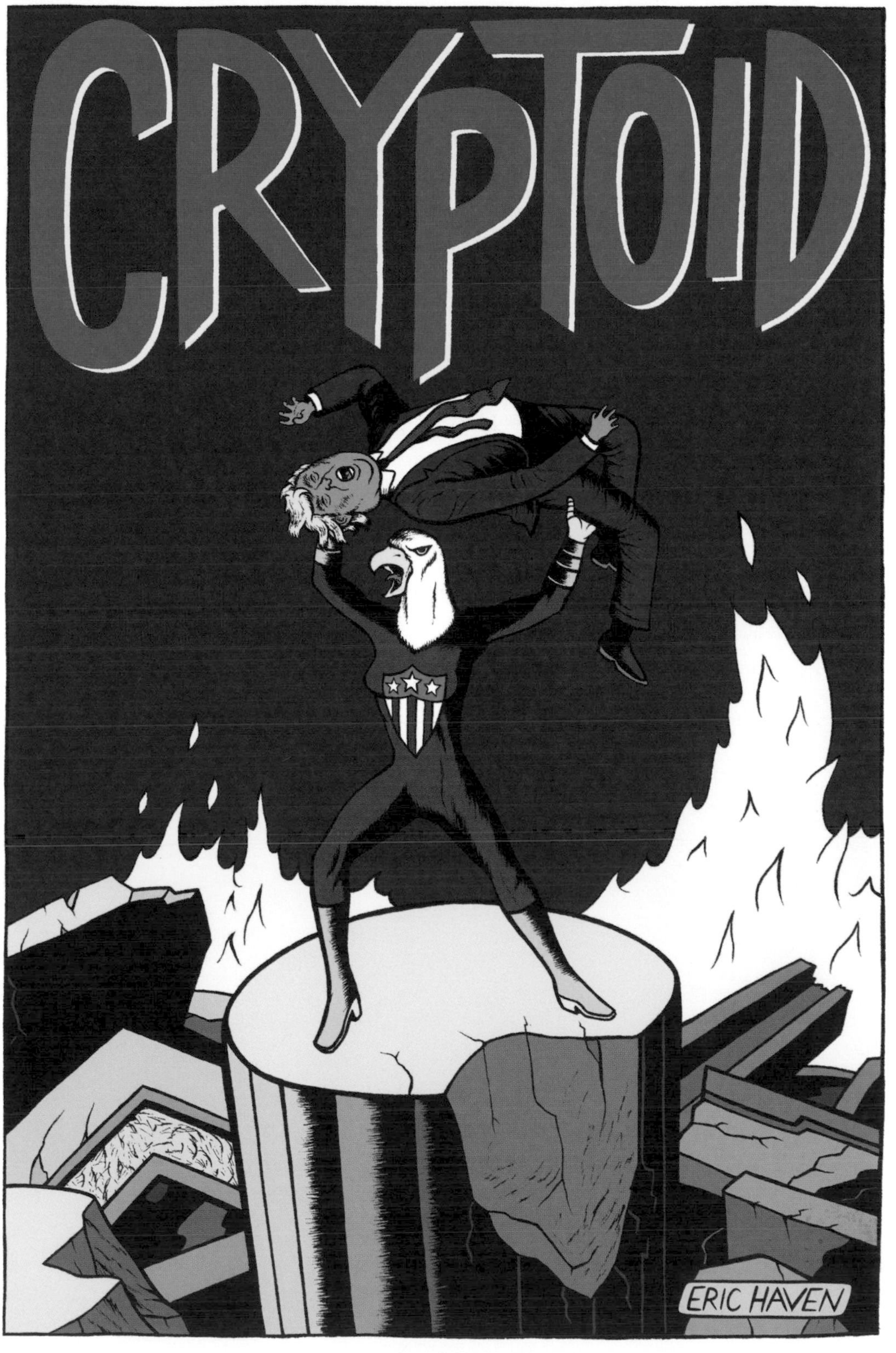
CRYPTOID
ERIC HAVEN

FANTAGRAPHICS BOOKS INC. 7563 LAKE CITY WAY NE SEATTLE, WA 98115
EDITOR AND ASSOCIATE PUBLISHER: ERIC REYNOLDS
BOOK DESIGN: ERIC HAVEN
PRODUCTION: PAUL BARESH
PUBLISHER: GARY GROTH
LIBRARY OF CONGRESS CONTROL NUMBER: 2019944673
ISBN: 978-1-68396-278-6
THANKS: RINA, BEN, RICHARD, DAN, AND ESPECIALLY DIANA, FOREVER.
FIRST PRINTING: FEBRUARY 2020
PRINTED IN CHINA.
DEDICATED TO MATT PLUMB — PAINTER, TEACHER, COMPADRE.

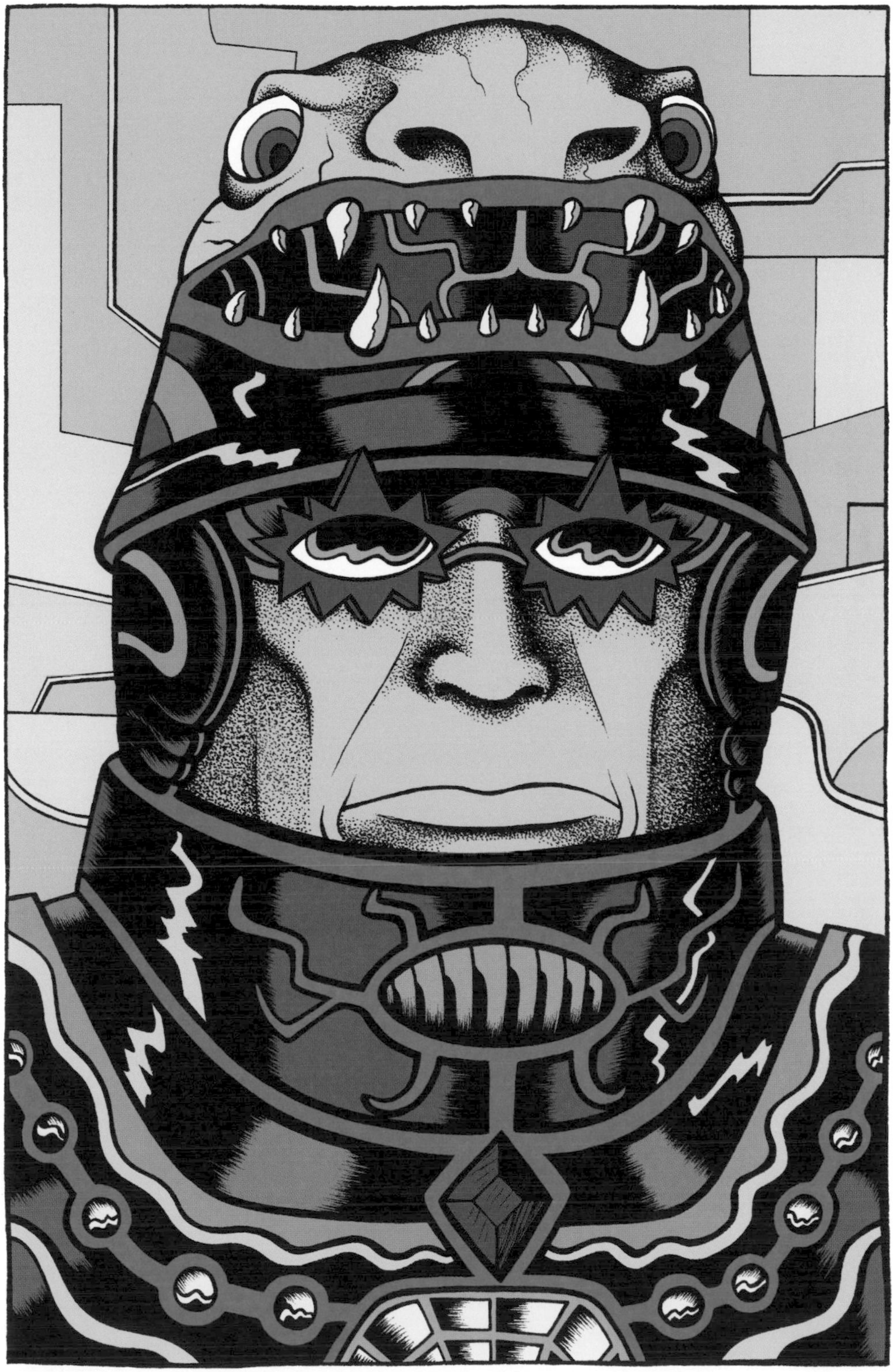

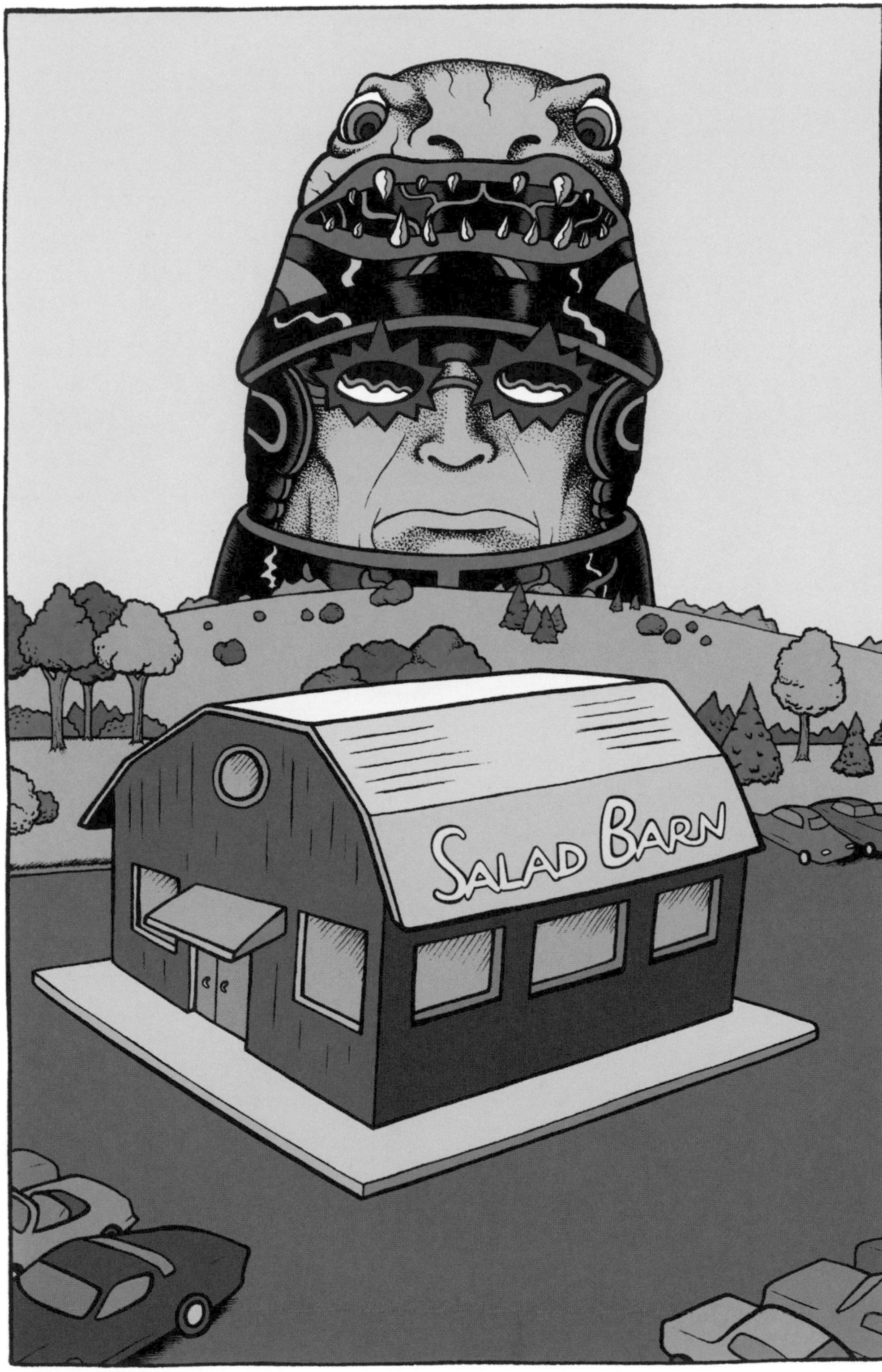
SALAD BARN

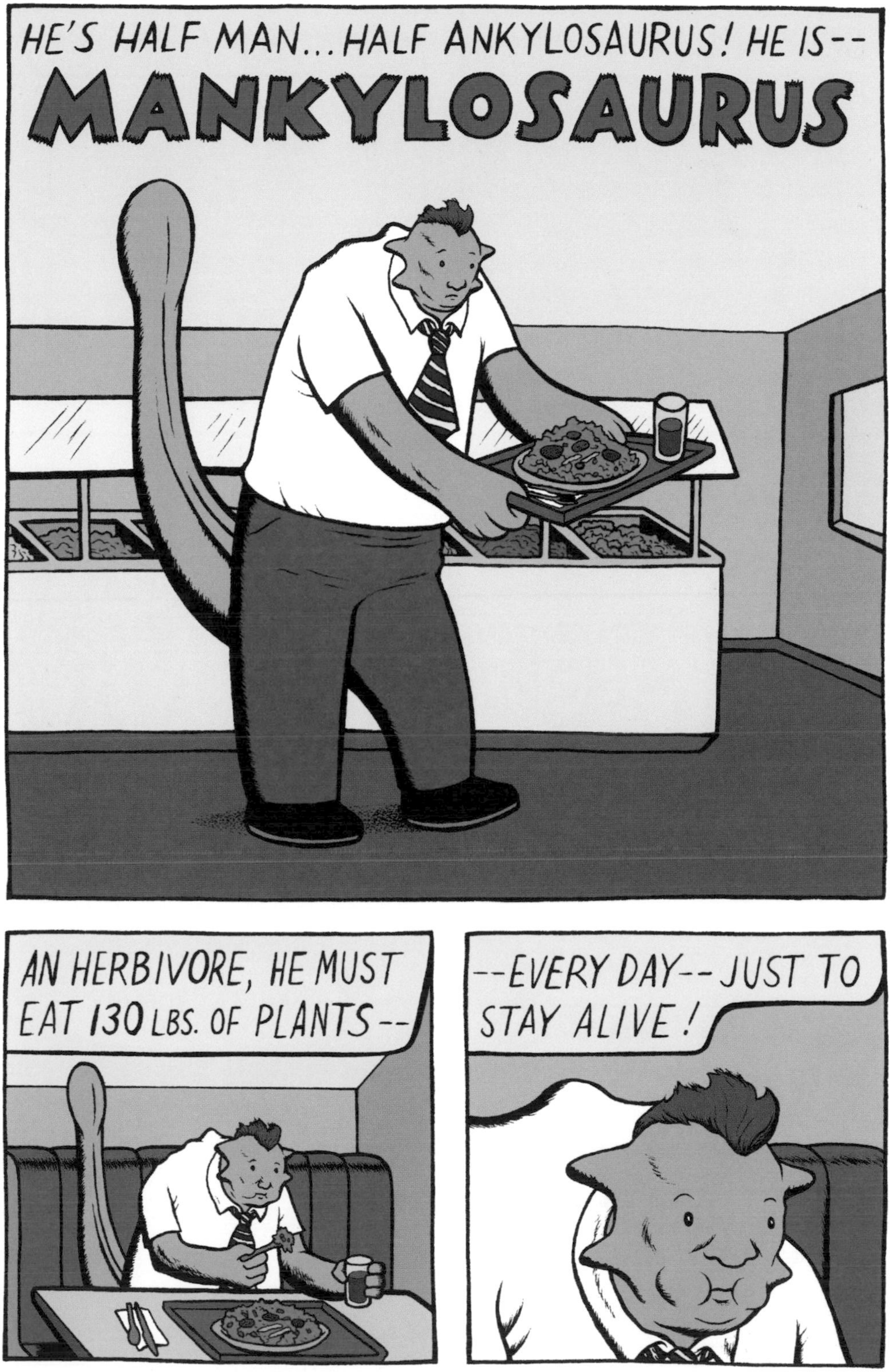
HE'S HALF MAN...HALF ANKYLOSAURUS! HE IS--
MANKYLOSAURUS
AN HERBIVORE, HE MUST EAT 130 LBS. OF PLANTS--
--EVERY DAY-- JUST TO STAY ALIVE!

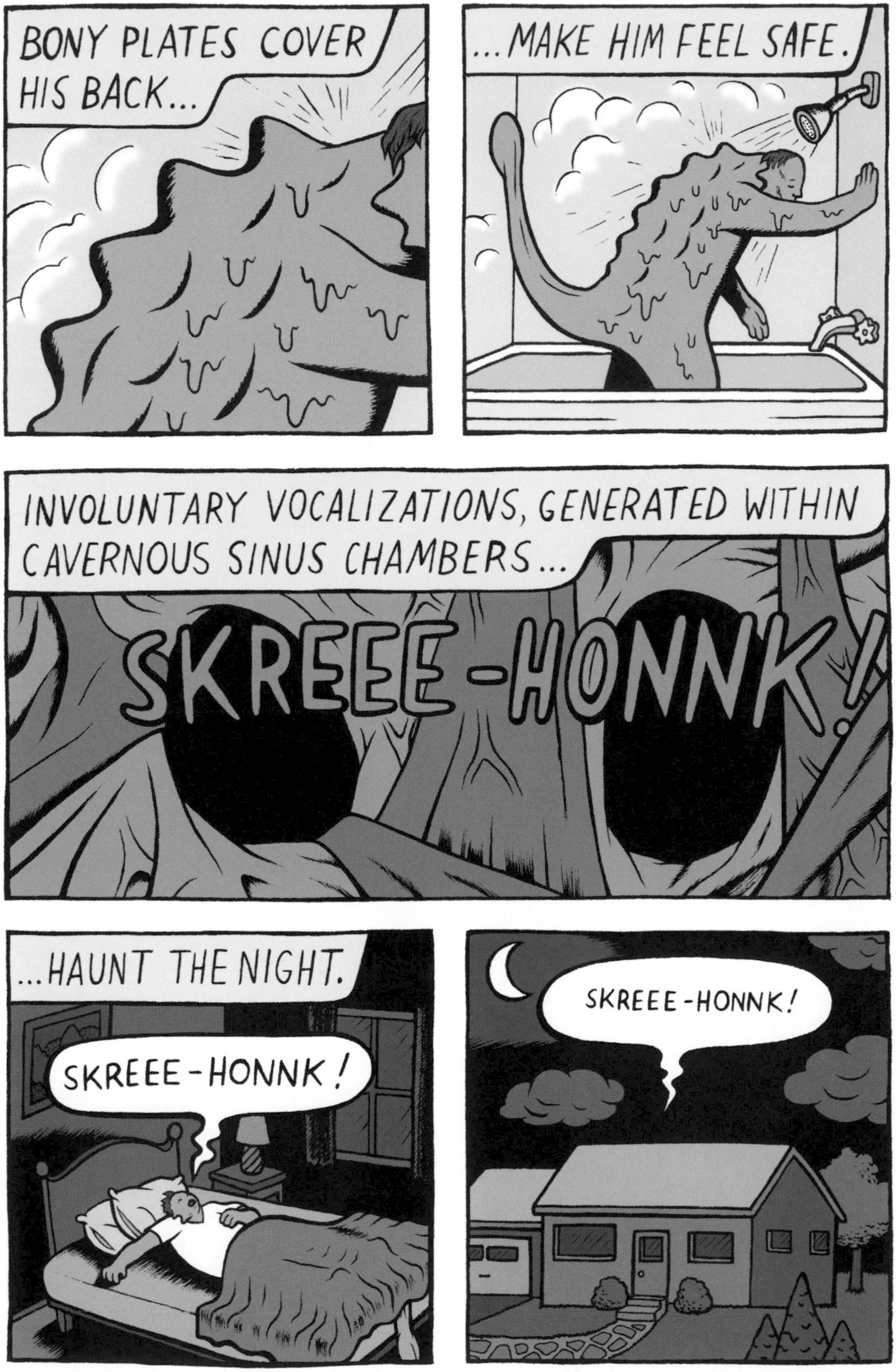
BONY PLATES COVER HIS BACK...
...MAKE HIM FEEL SAFE.
INVOLUNTARY VOCALIZATIONS, GENERATED WITHIN CAVERNOUS SINUS CHAMBERS...
SKREEE-HONNK!
...HAUNT THE NIGHT.
SKREEE-HONNK!
SKREEE-HONNK!

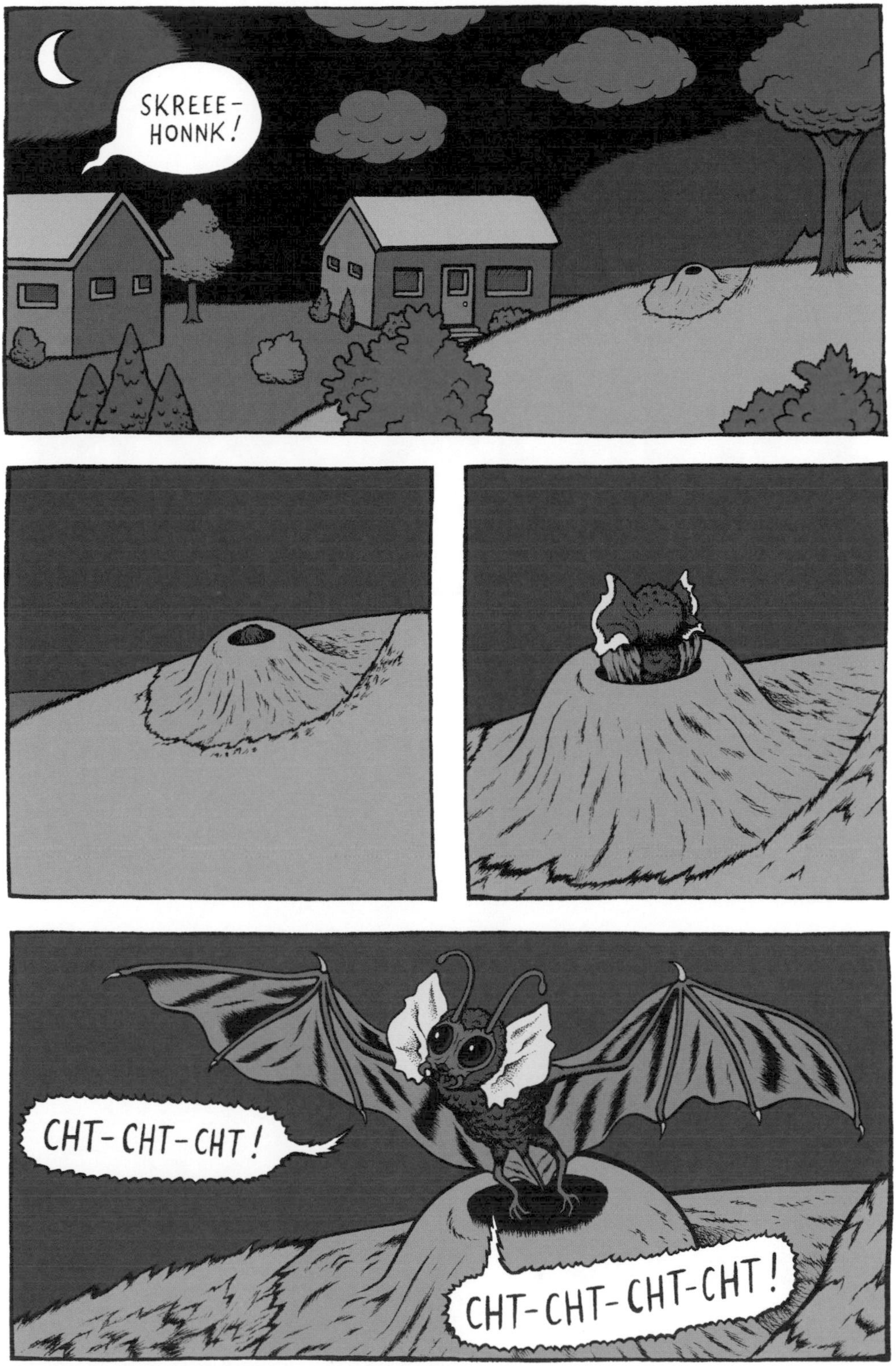
SKREEE-
HONNK!
CHT-CHT-CHT!
CHT-CHT-CHT-CHT!

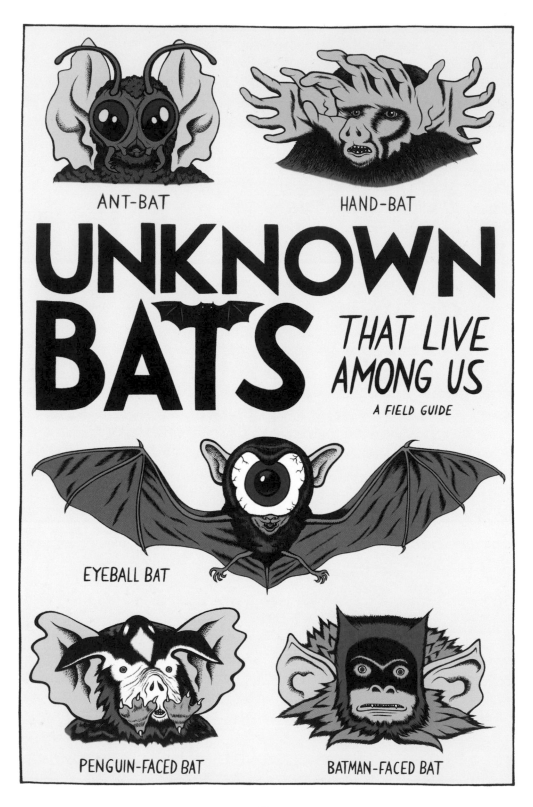

ANT-BAT

HAND-BAT

UNKNOWN BATS

THAT LIVE AMONG US

A FIELD GUIDE

EYEBALL BAT

PENGUIN-FACED BAT

BATMAN-FACED BAT

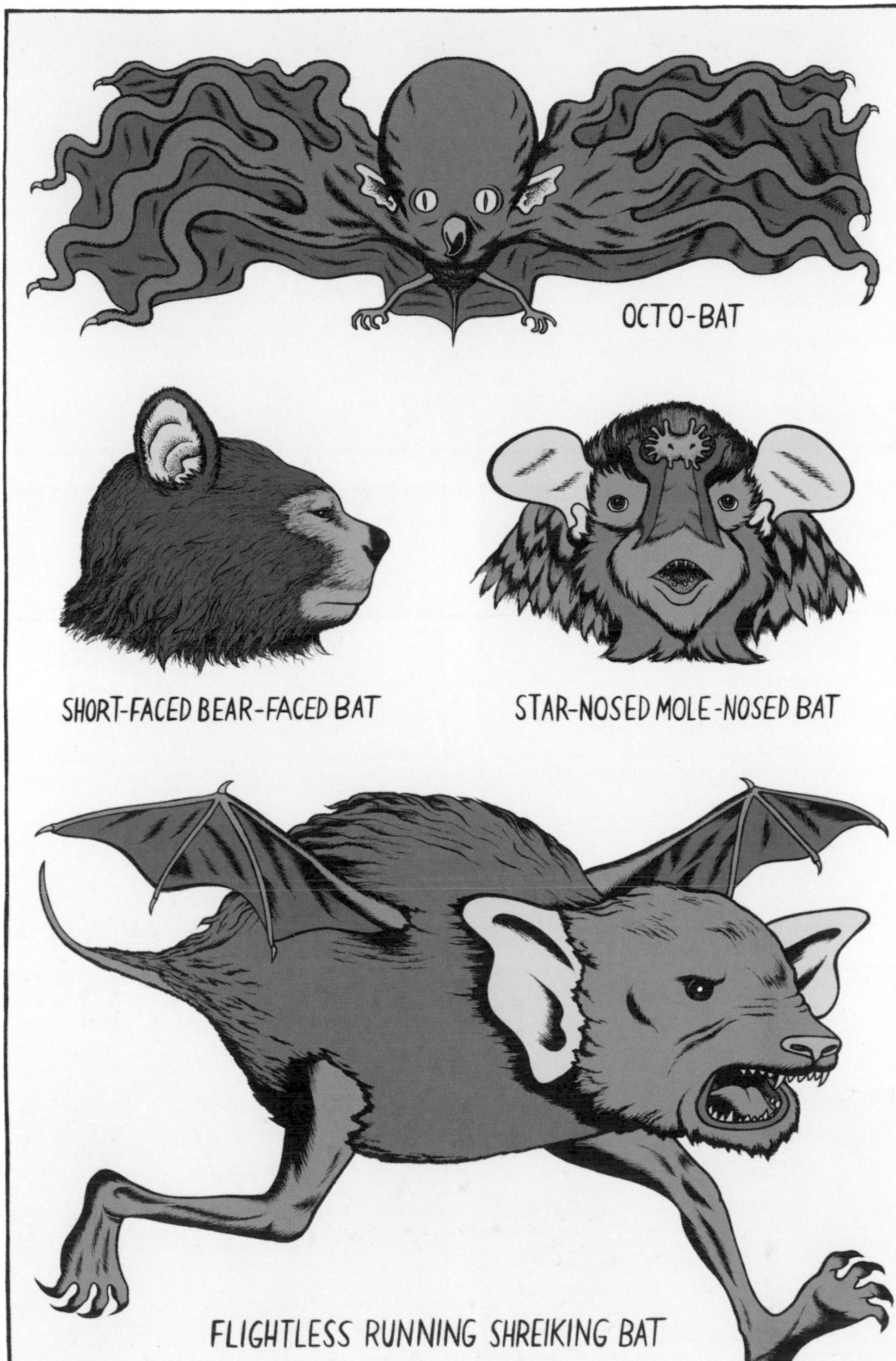
OCTO-BAT
SHORT-FACED BEAR-FACED BAT
STAR-NOSED MOLE-NOSED BAT
FLIGHTLESS RUNNING SHREIKING BAT

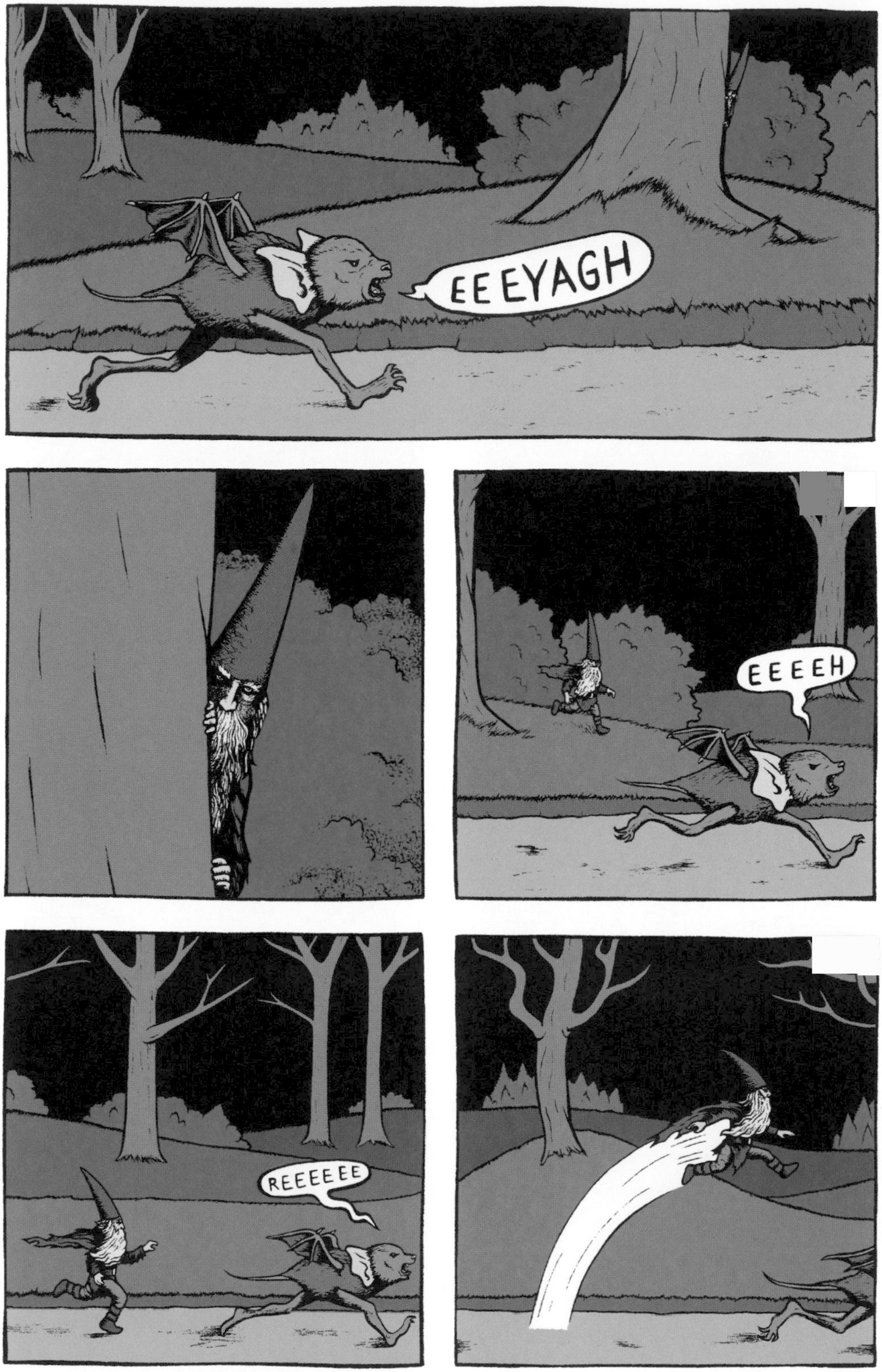
EEEYAGH
EEEEH
REEEEEE

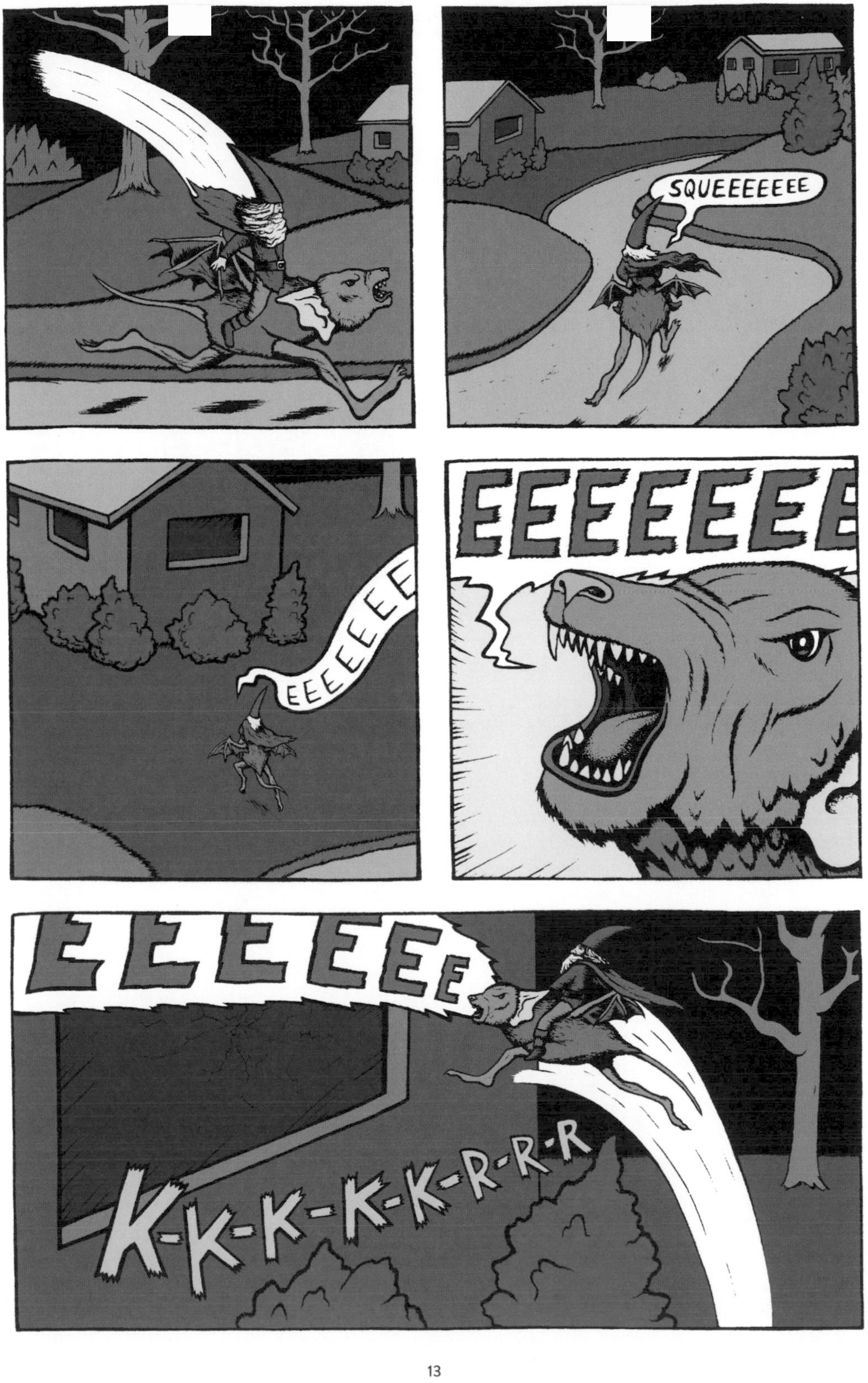
SQUEEEEEEE
EEEEEEEE
EEEEEEE
EEEEEe
K-K-K-K-K-R-R-R

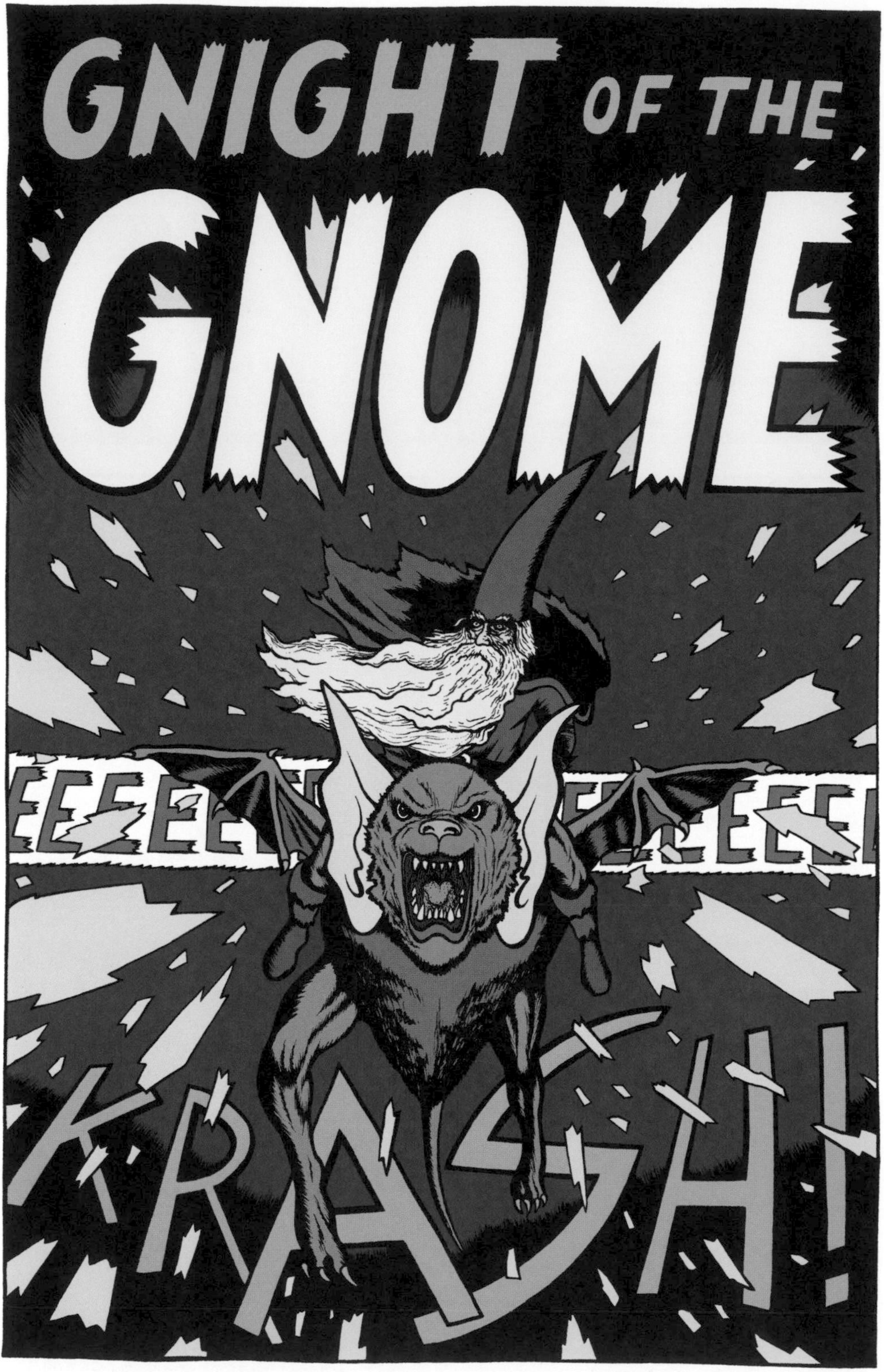
GNIGHT OF THE
GNOME
EEEEEEEEEE
KRAAGH!

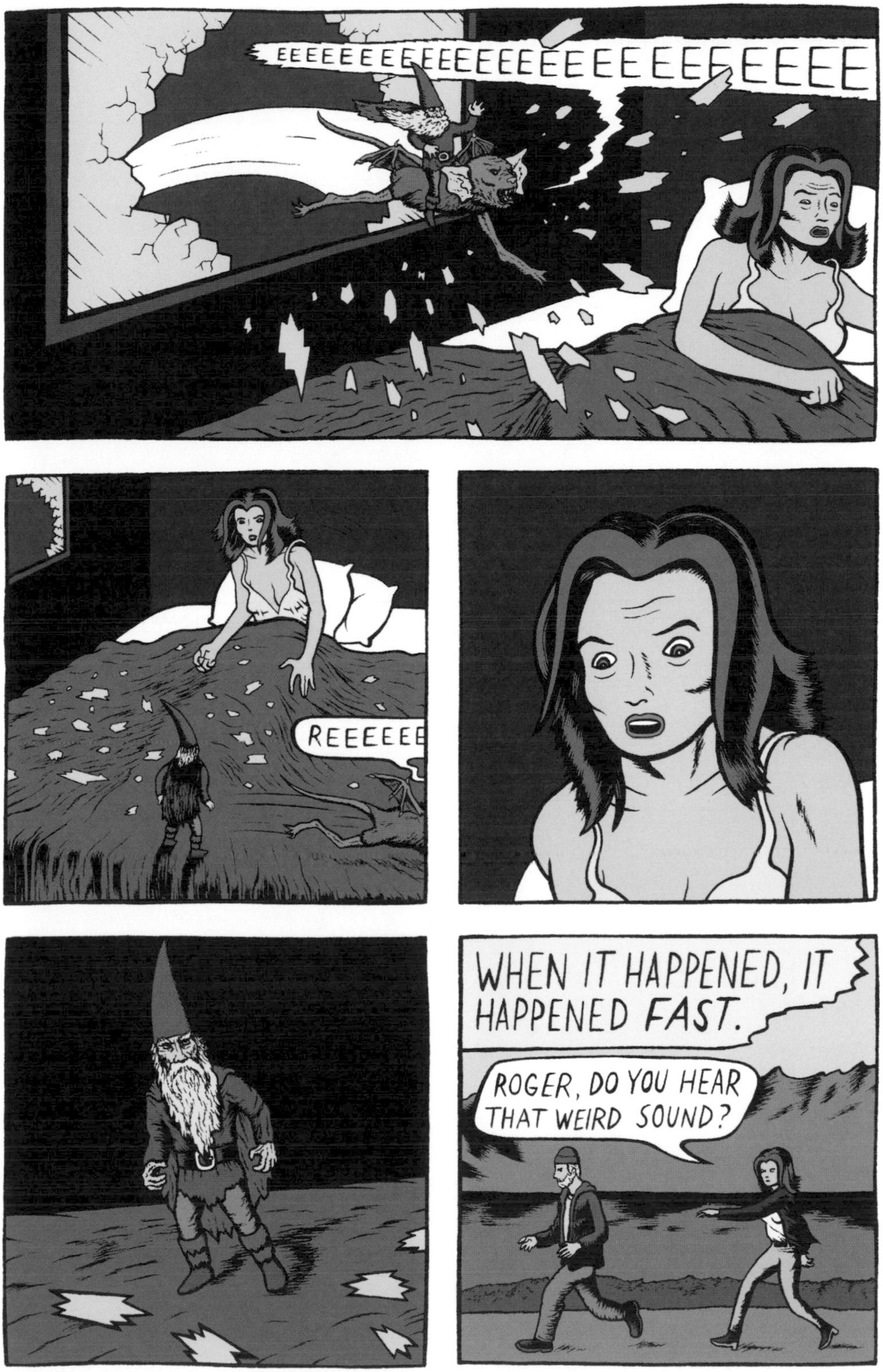
EEEEEEEEEEEEEEEEEEEEEEEEE
REEEEEE
WHEN IT HAPPENED, IT HAPPENED FAST.
ROGER, DO YOU HEAR THAT WEIRD SOUND?

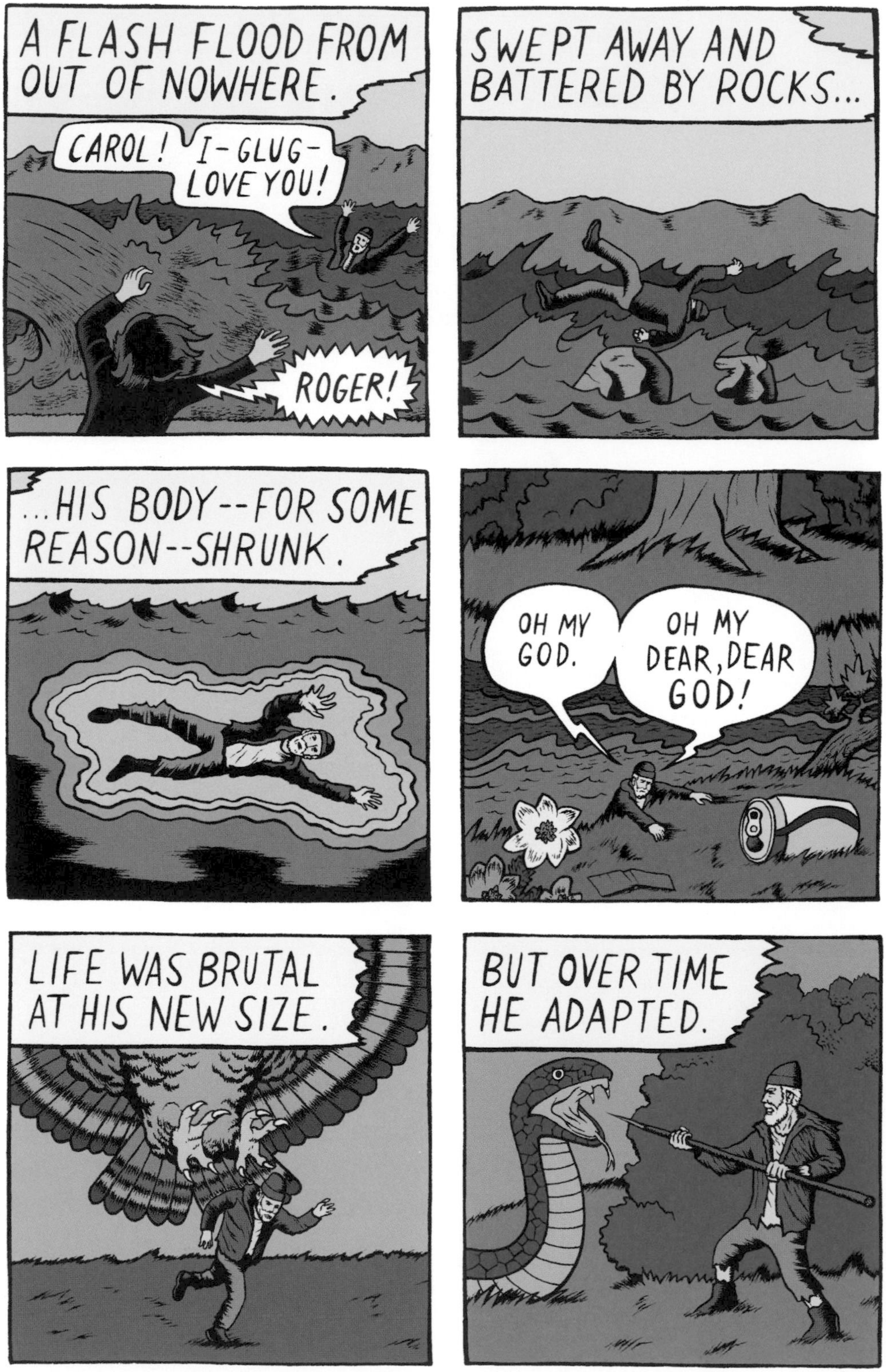
A FLASH FLOOD FROM OUT OF NOWHERE.
CAROL!
I-GLUG-LOVE YOU!
ROGER!
SWEPT AWAY AND BATTERED BY ROCKS...
...HIS BODY--FOR SOME REASON--SHRUNK.
OH MY GOD.
OH MY DEAR, DEAR GOD!
LIFE WAS BRUTAL AT HIS NEW SIZE.
BUT OVER TIME HE ADAPTED.

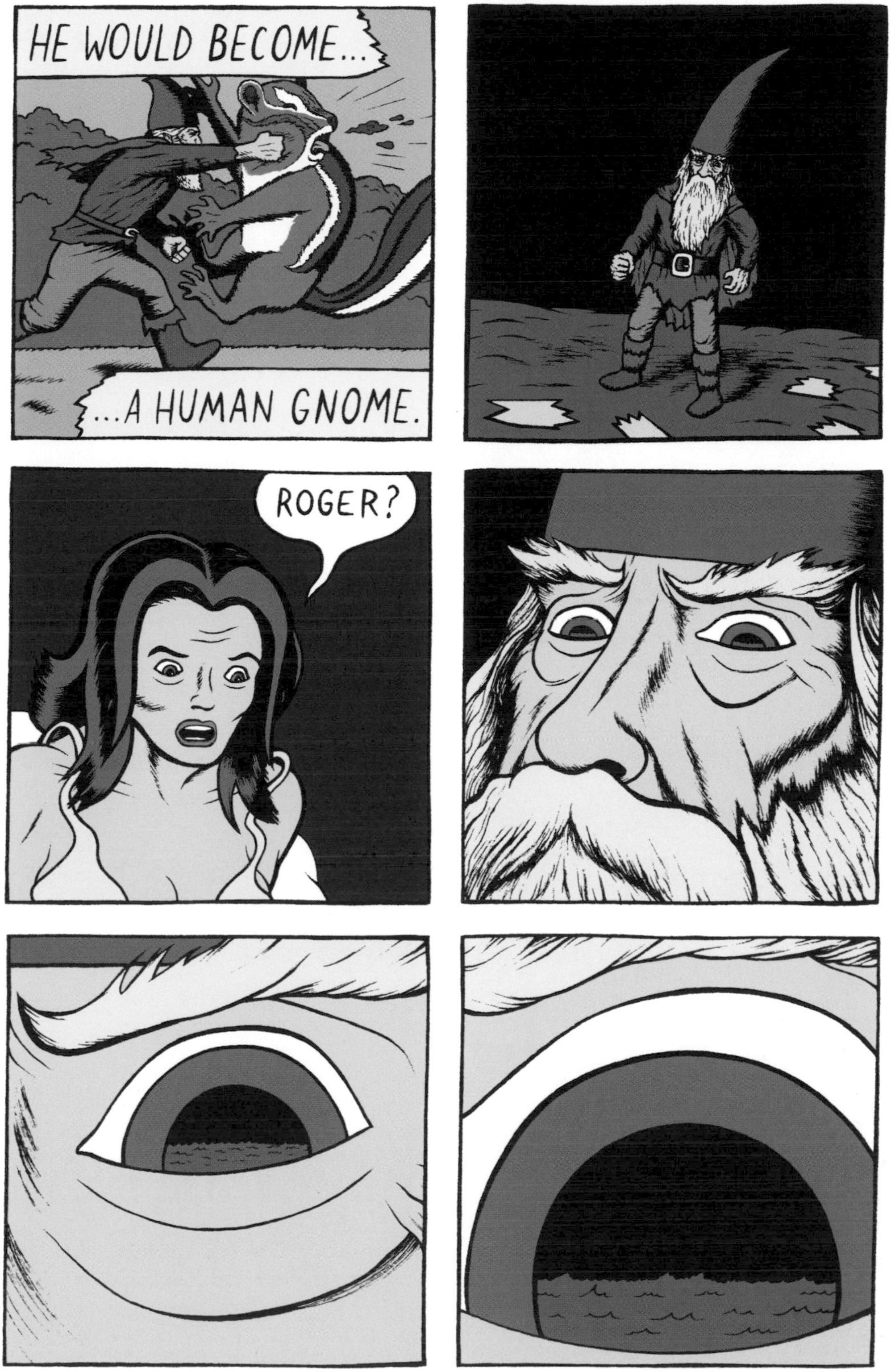
HE WOULD BECOME...
...A HUMAN GNOME.
ROGER?

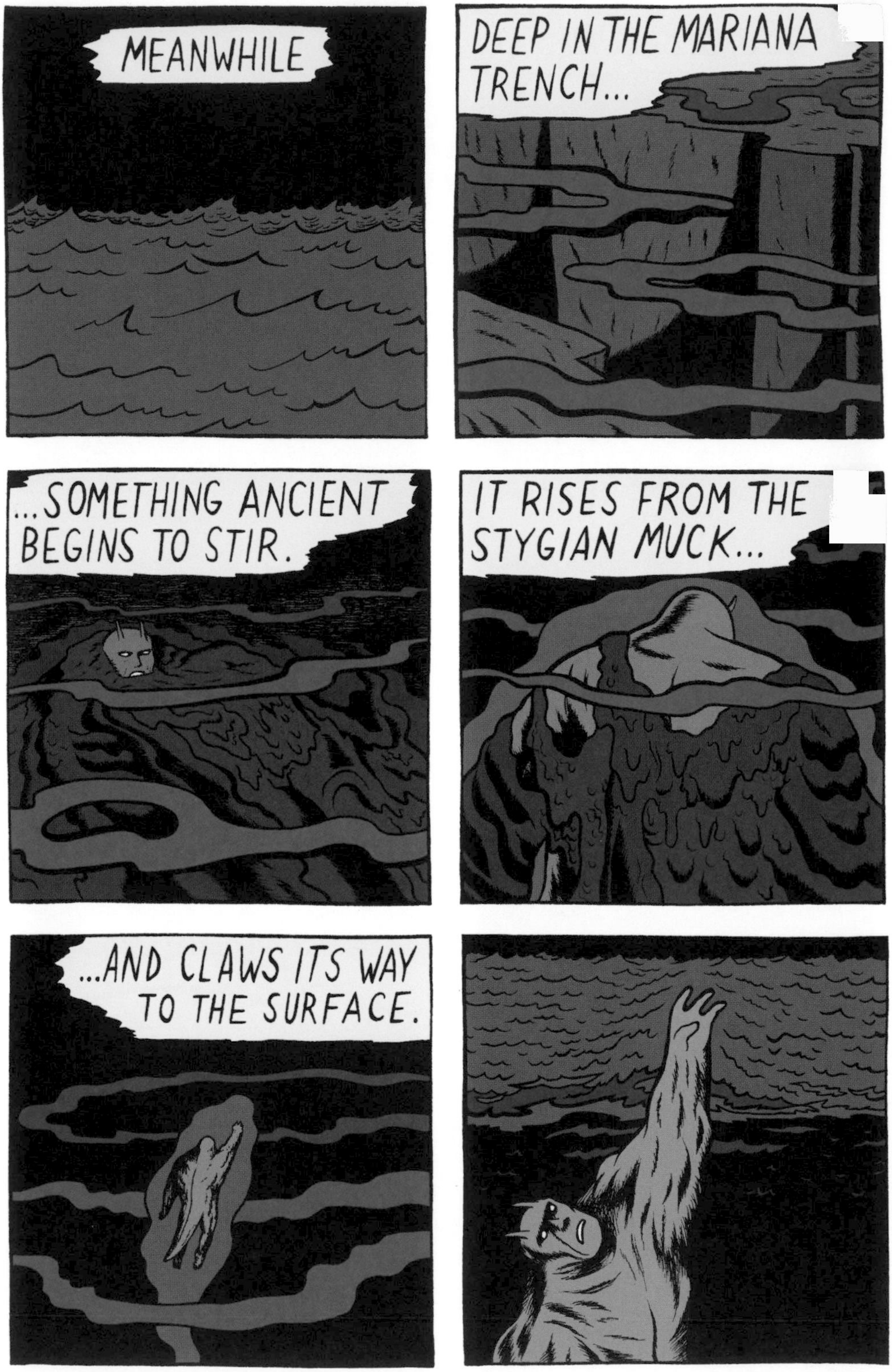
MEANWHILE
DEEP IN THE MARIANA TRENCH...
...SOMETHING ANCIENT BEGINS TO STIR.
IT RISES FROM THE STYGIAN MUCK...
...AND CLAWS ITS WAY TO THE SURFACE.

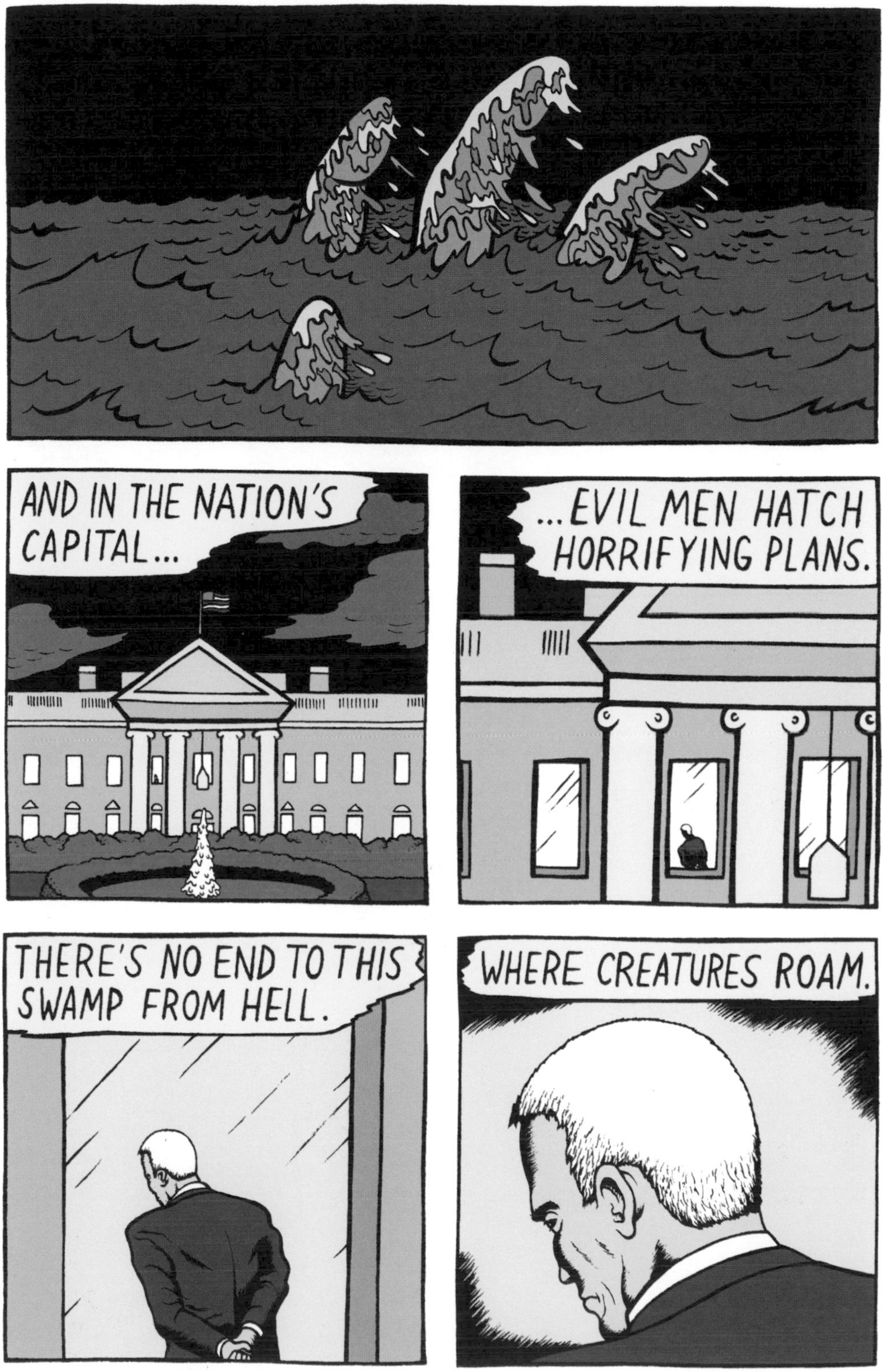
AND IN THE NATION'S CAPITAL...
...EVIL MEN HATCH HORRIFYING PLANS.
THERE'S NO END TO THIS SWAMP FROM HELL.
WHERE CREATURES ROAM.

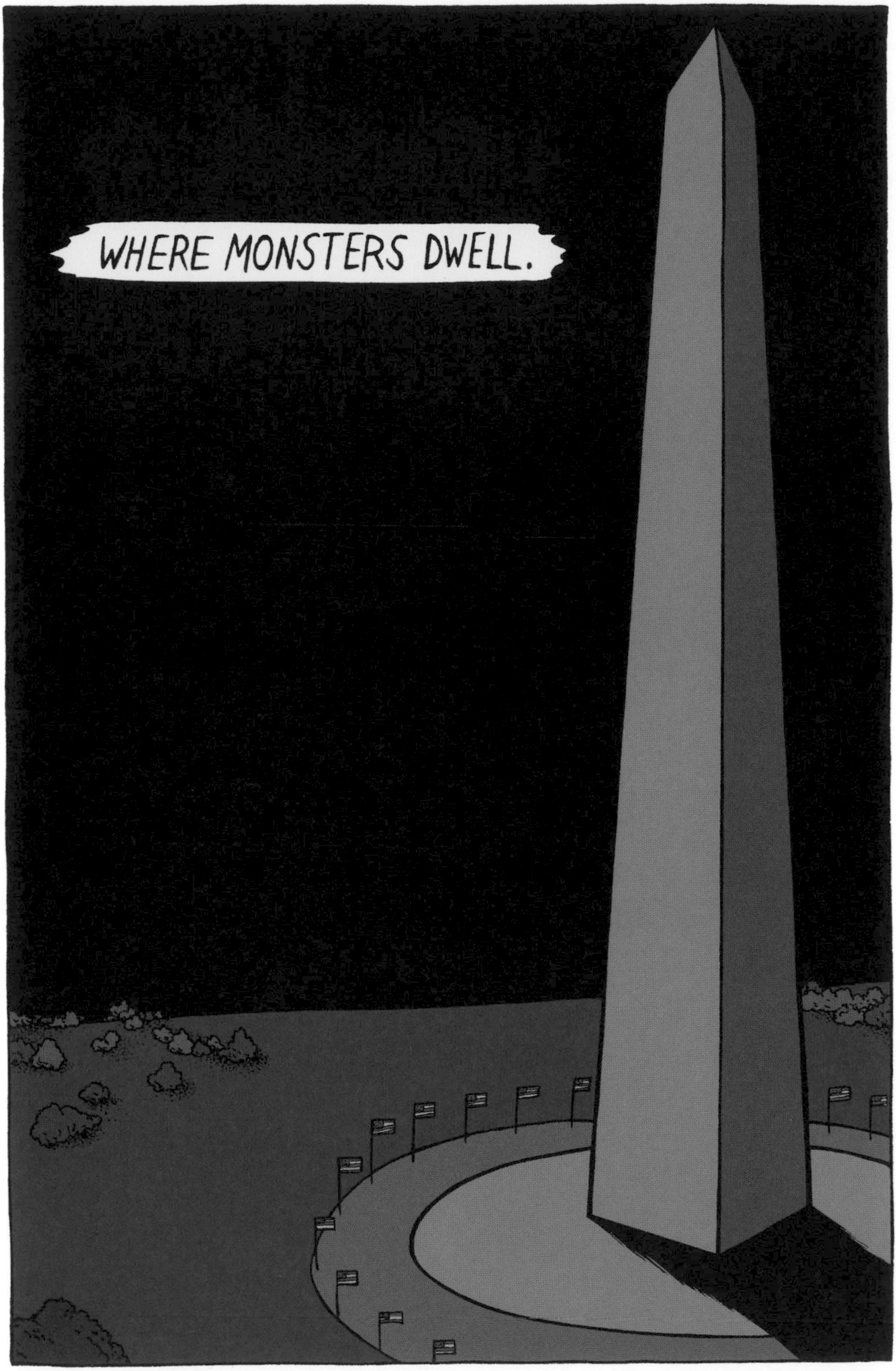
WHERE MONSTERS DWELL.

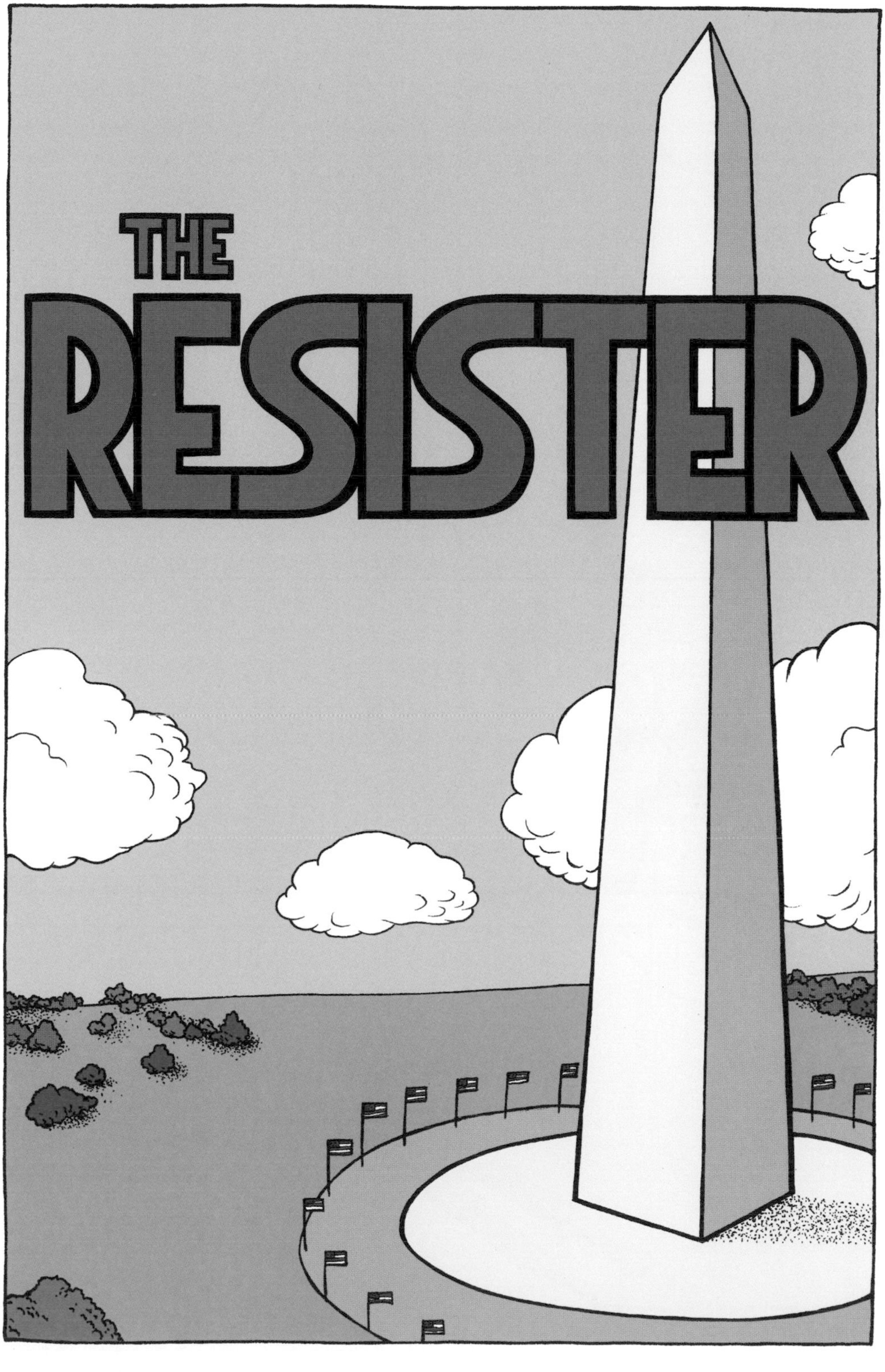
THE
RESISTER

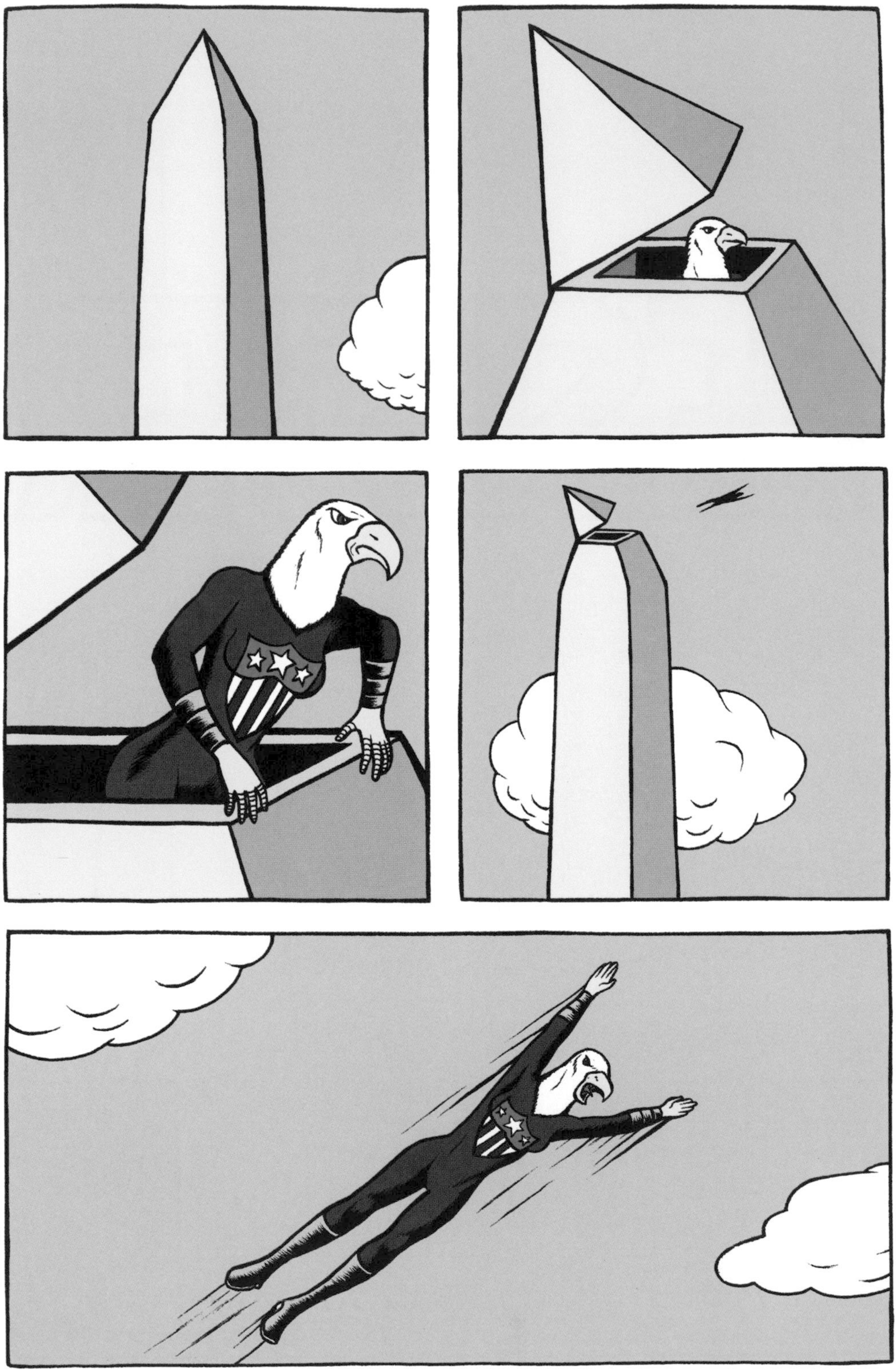

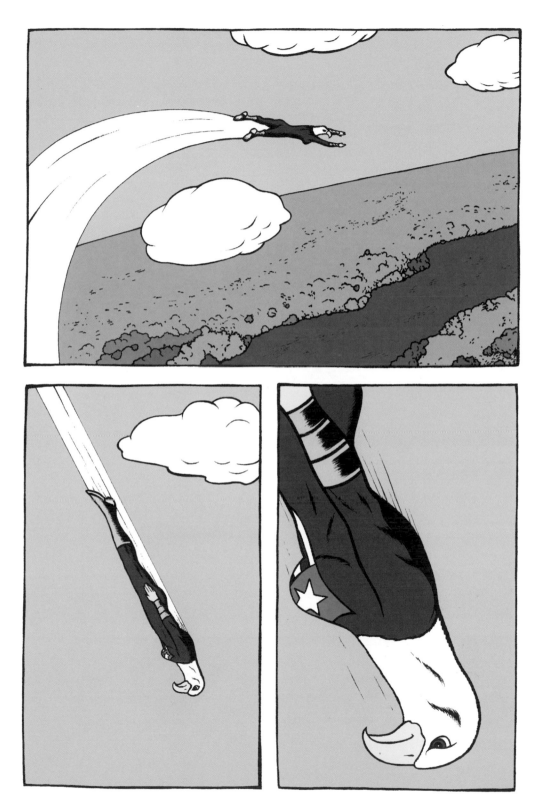

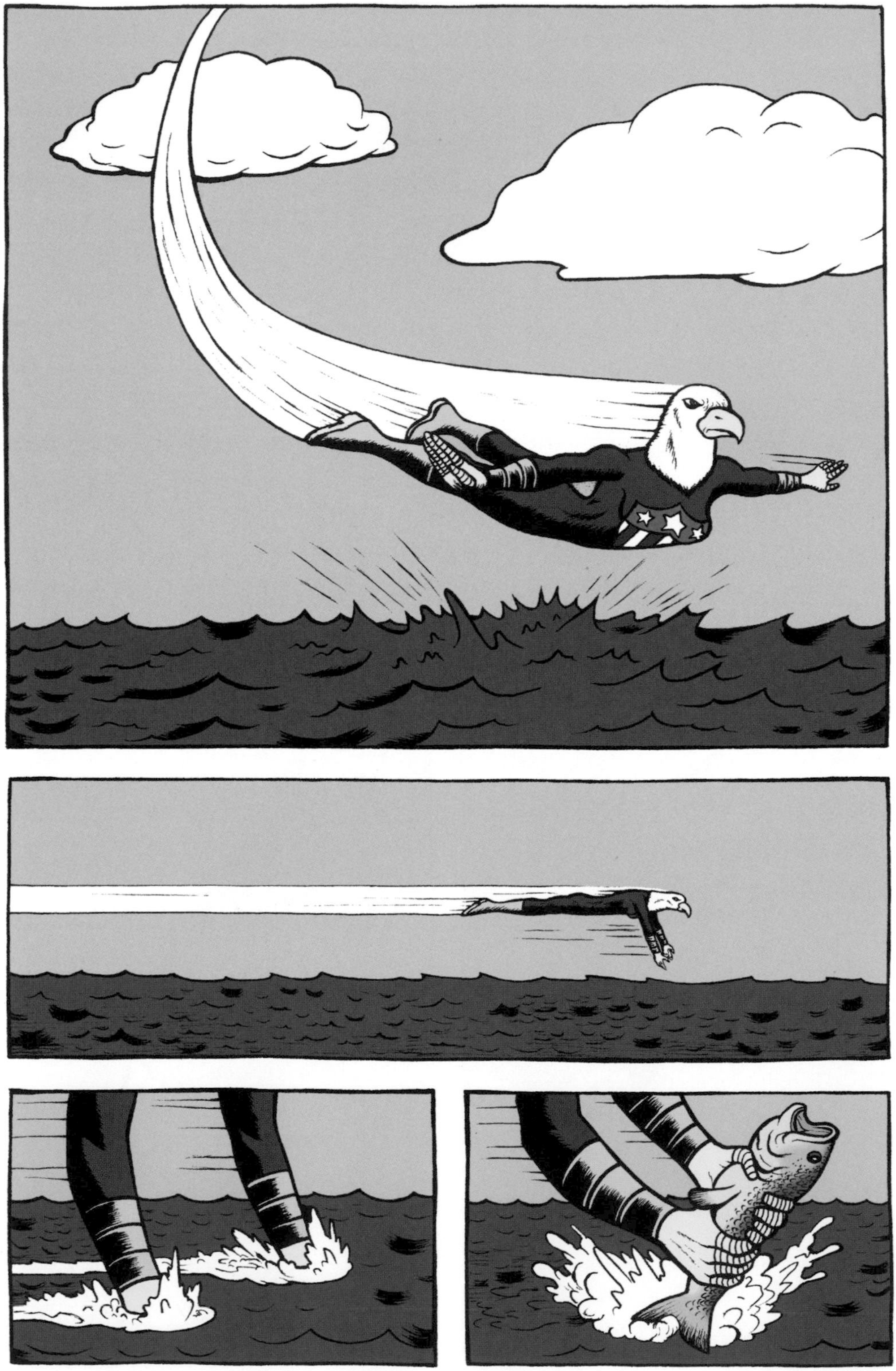

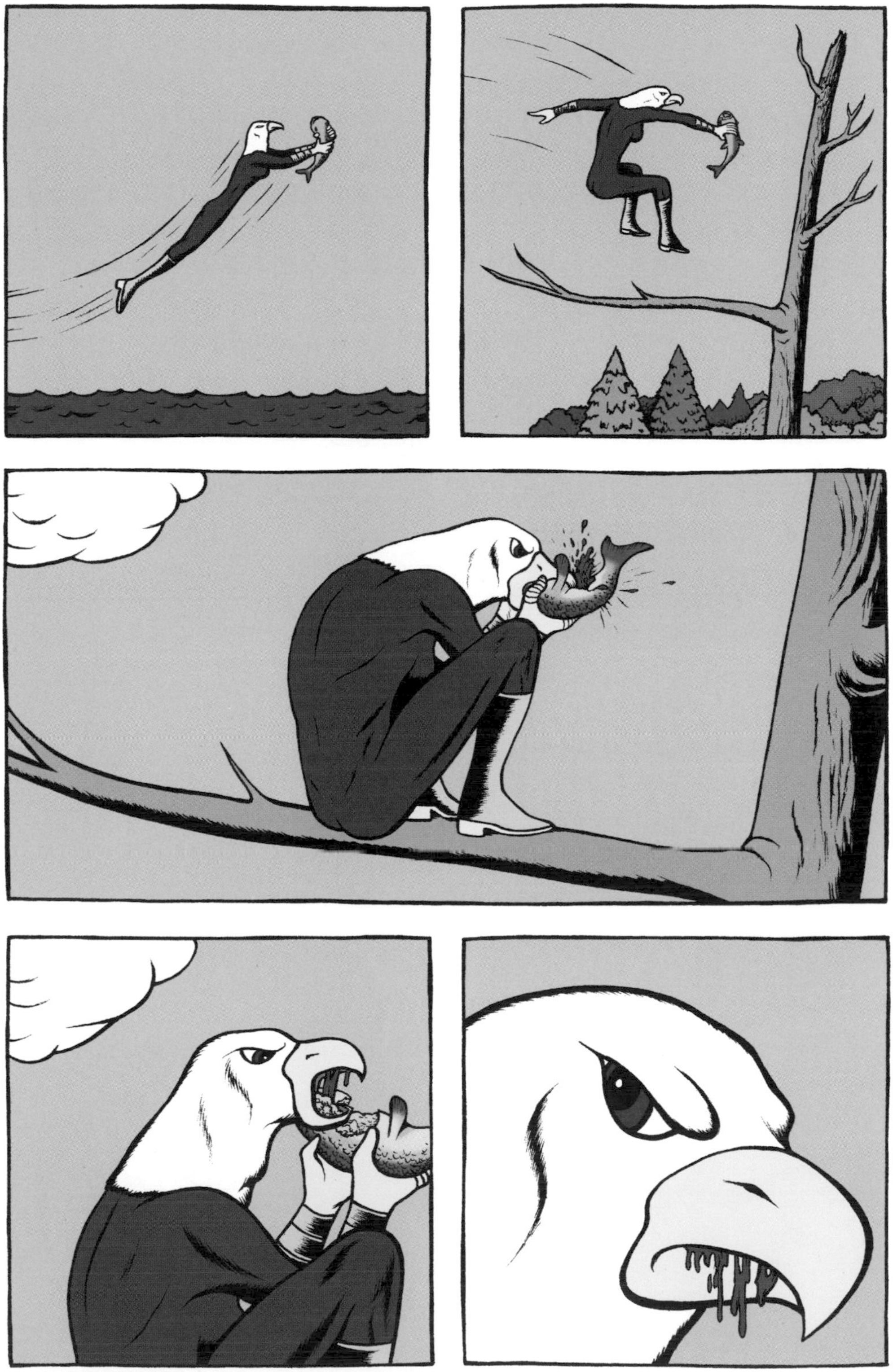

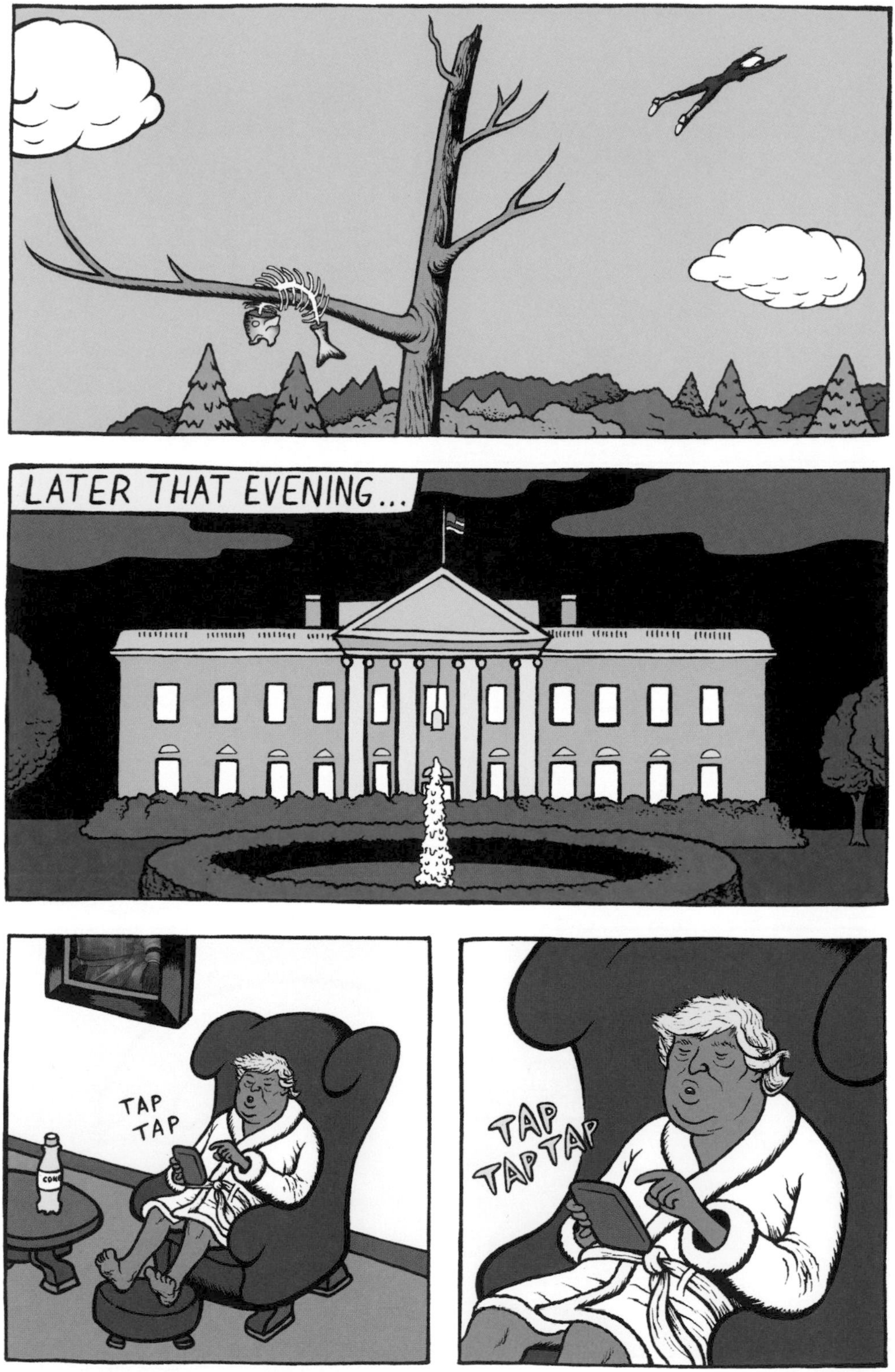
LATER THAT EVENING...
TAP
TAP
TAP
TAP TAP

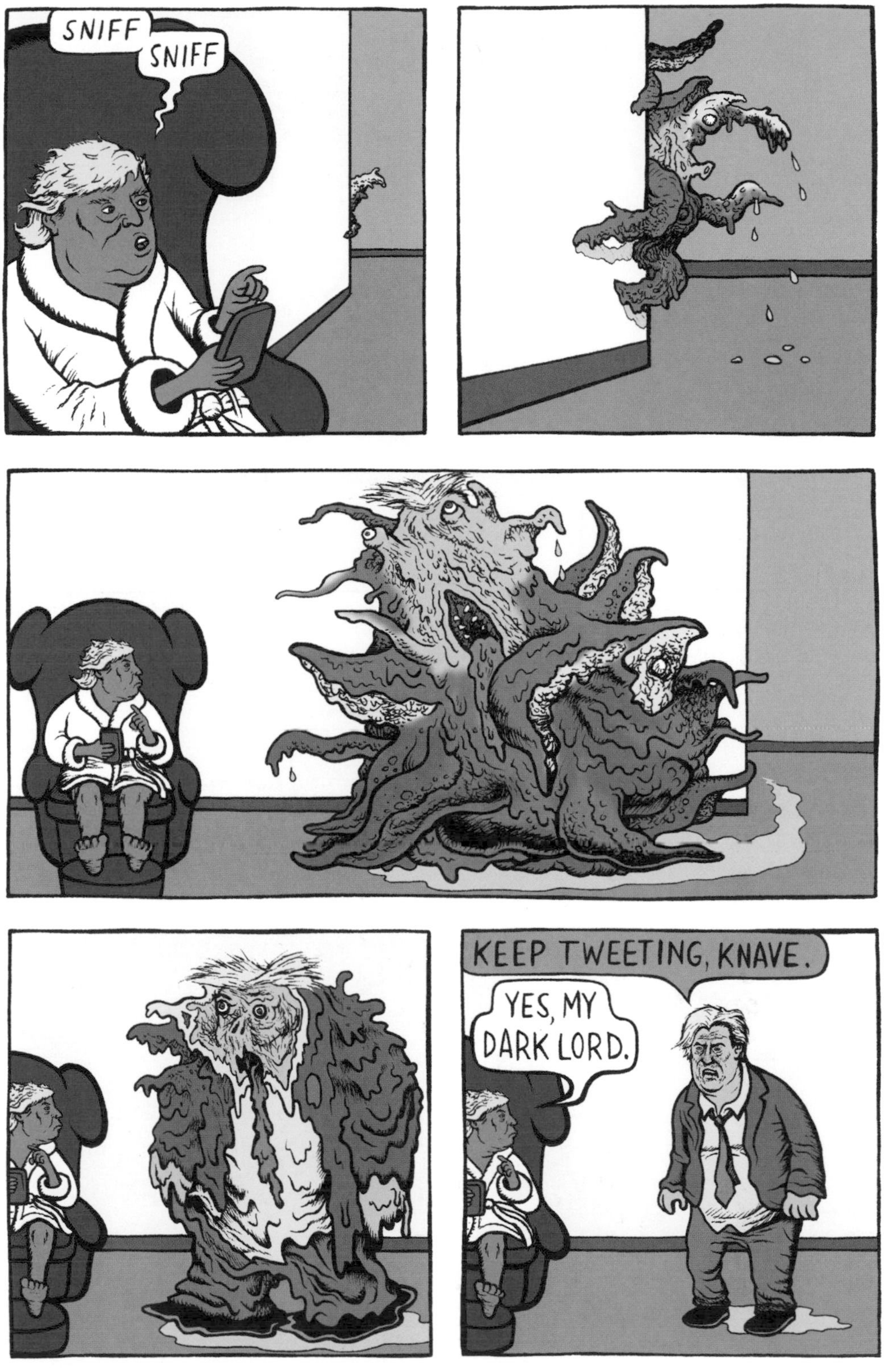
SNIFF
SNIFF
KEEP TWEETING, KNAVE.
YES, MY DARK LORD.

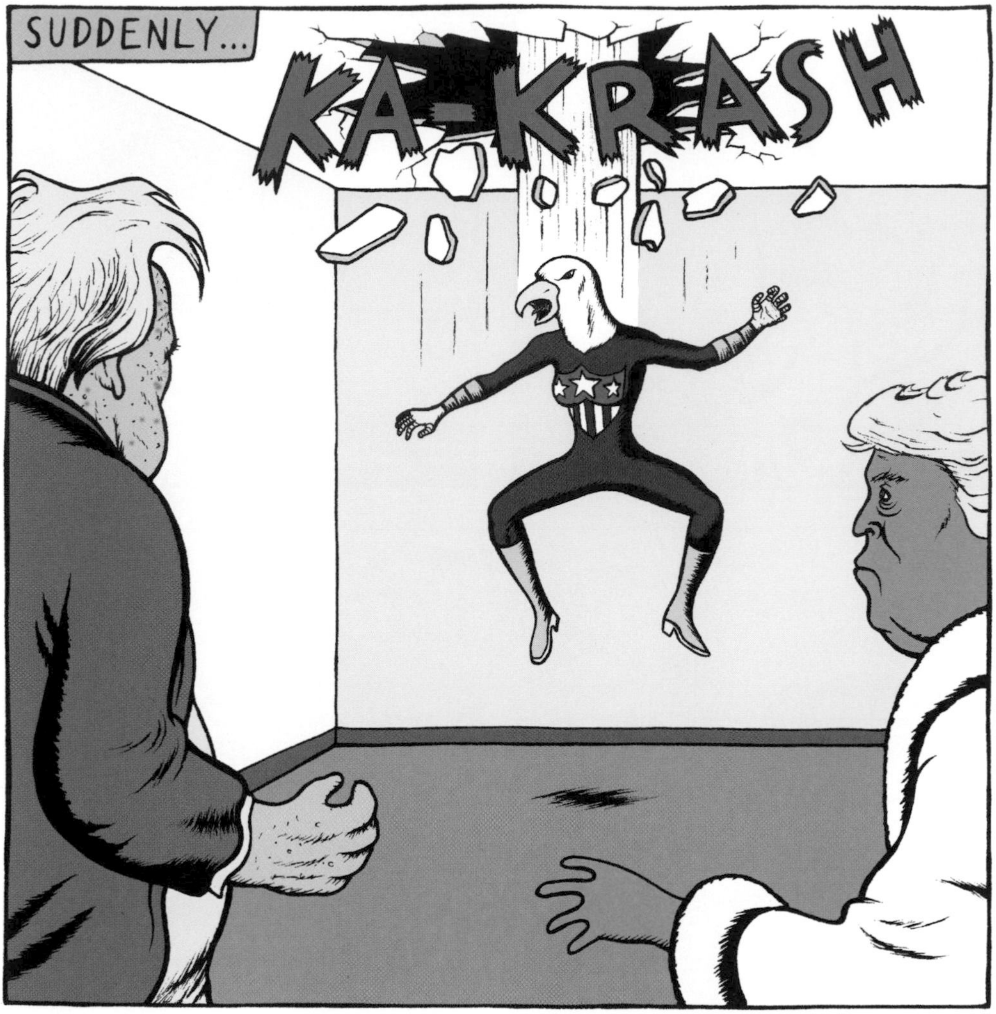
SUDDENLY...
KA-KRASH

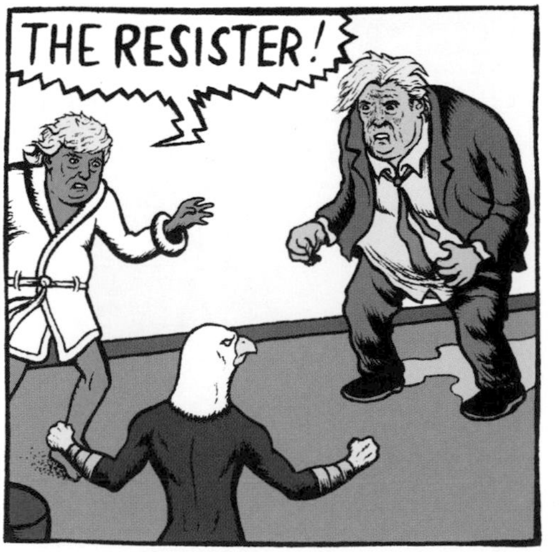
THE RESISTER!

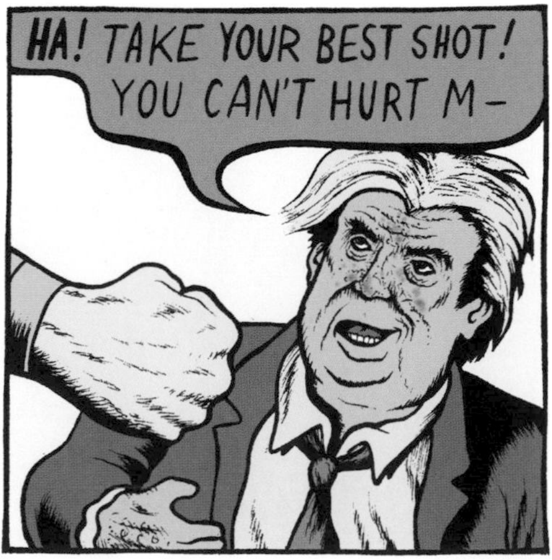
HA! TAKE YOUR BEST SHOT! YOU CAN'T HURT M-

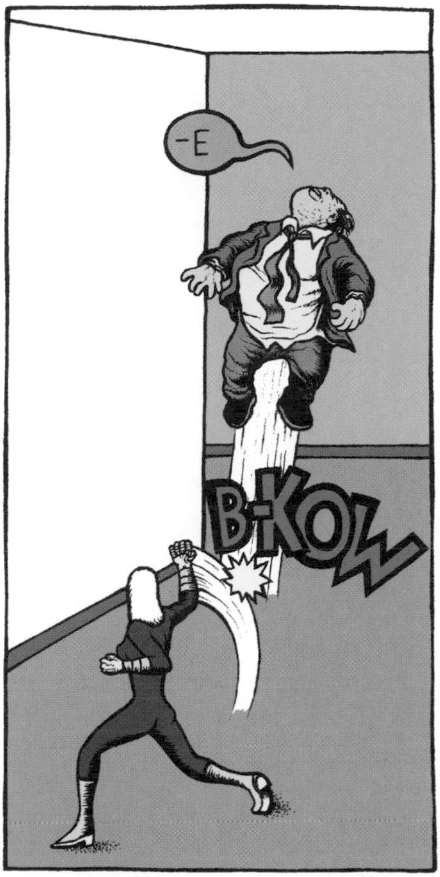
-E
B-KOW

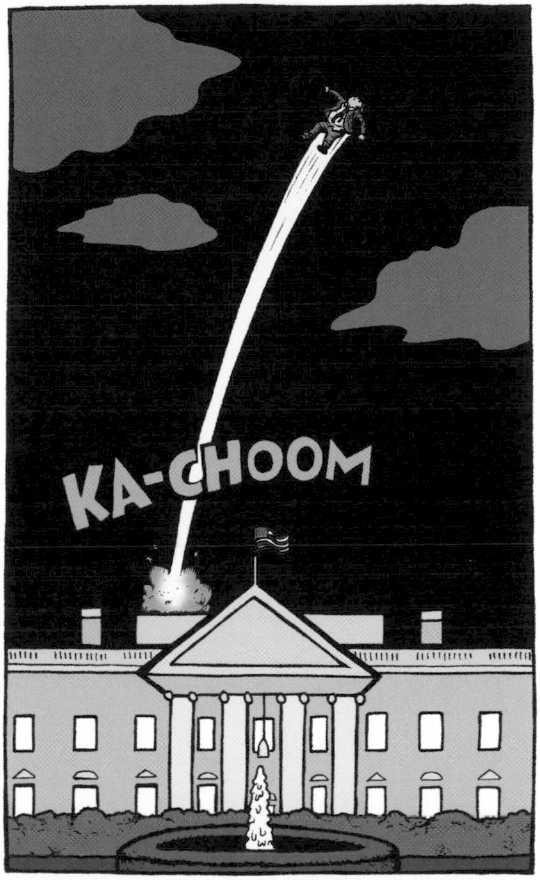
KA-CHOOM

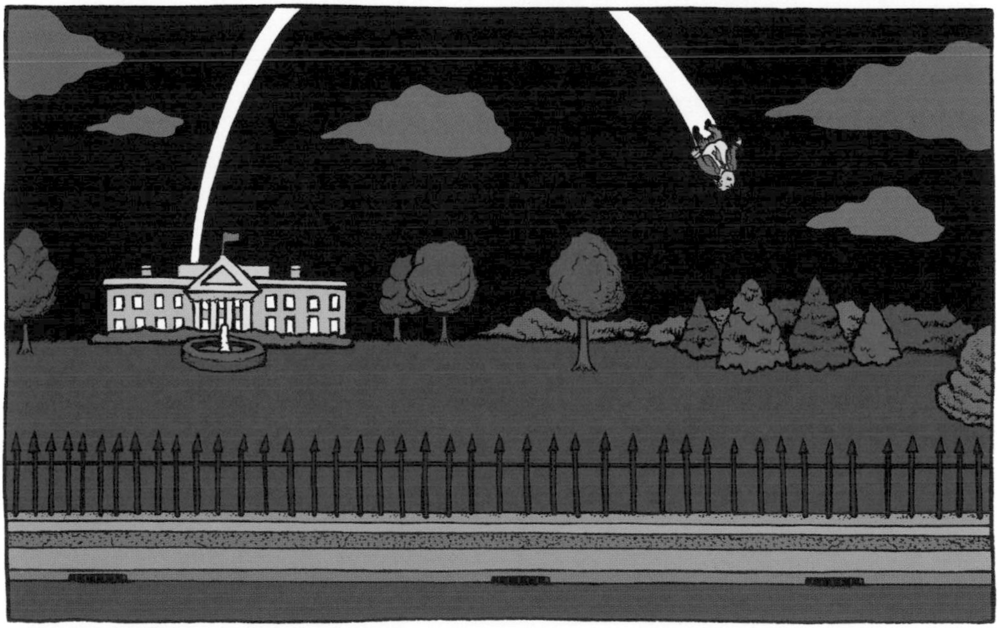

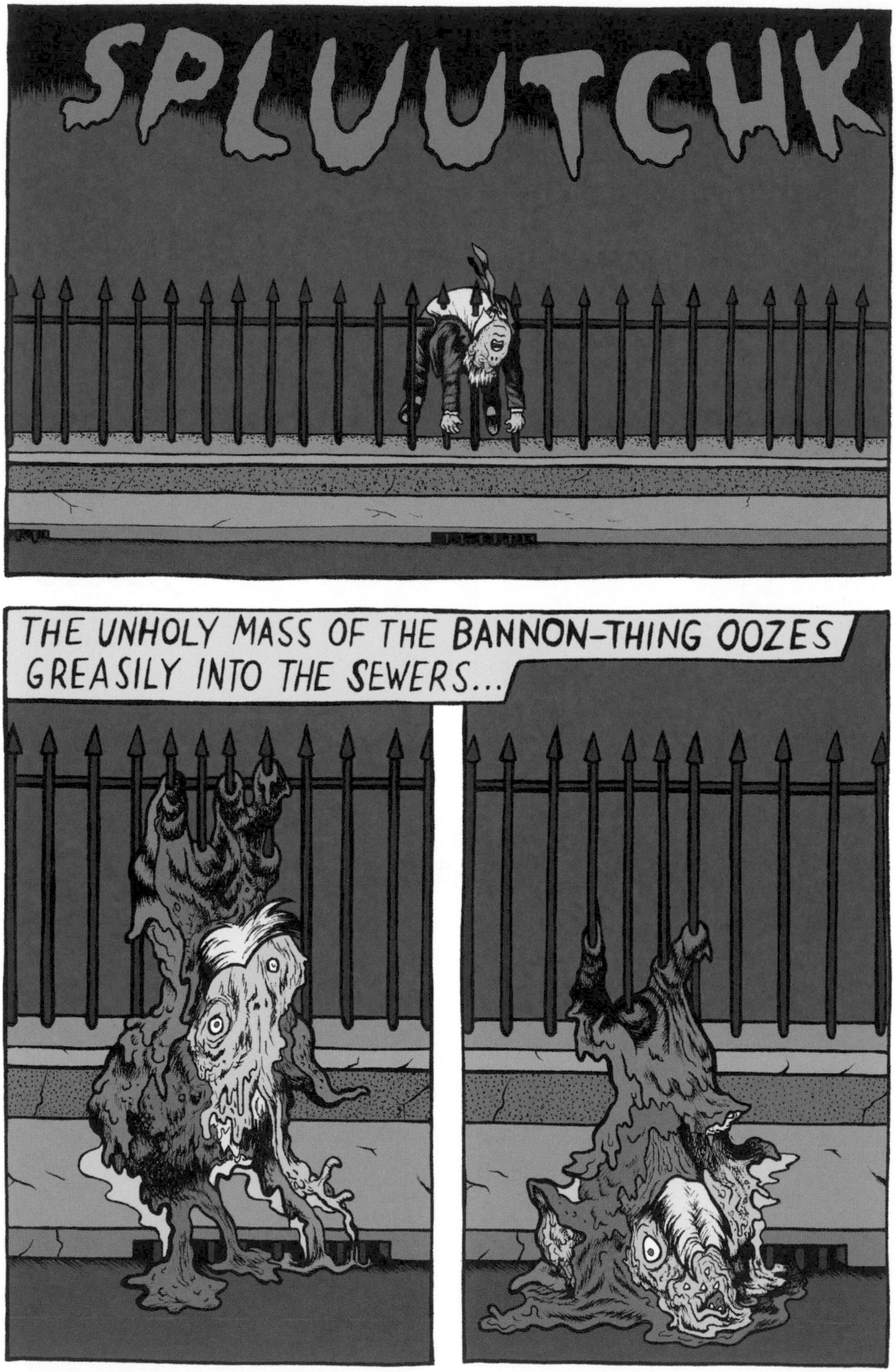
SPLUUTCHK
THE UNHOLY MASS OF THE BANNON-THING OOZES GREASILY INTO THE SEWERS...

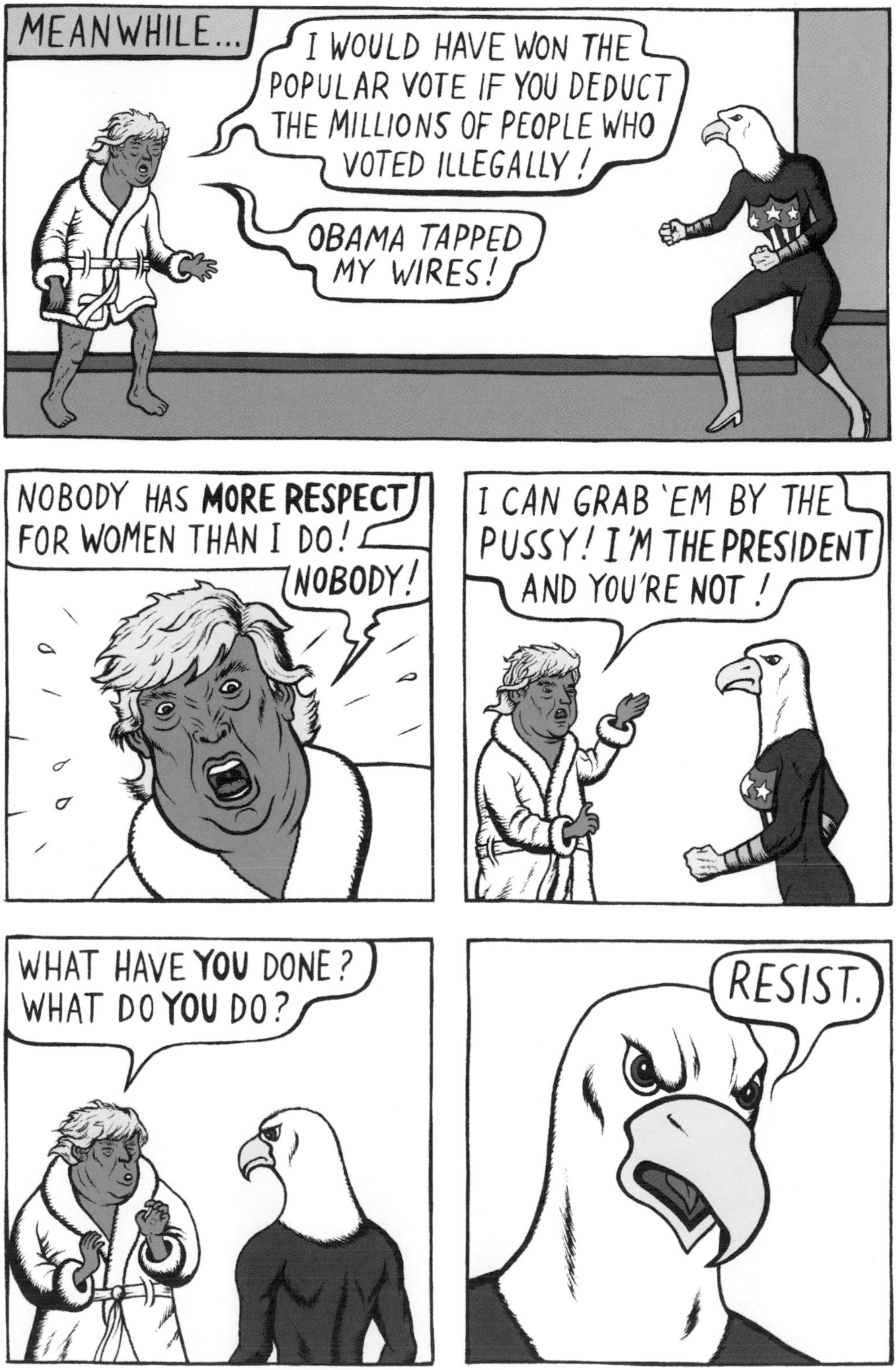
MEANWHILE...
I WOULD HAVE WON THE POPULAR VOTE IF YOU DEDUCT THE MILLIONS OF PEOPLE WHO VOTED ILLEGALLY!
OBAMA TAPPED MY WIRES!
NOBODY HAS MORE RESPECT FOR WOMEN THAN I DO!
NOBODY!
I CAN GRAB 'EM BY THE PUSSY! I'M THE PRESIDENT AND YOU'RE NOT!
WHAT HAVE YOU DONE? WHAT DO YOU DO?
RESIST.

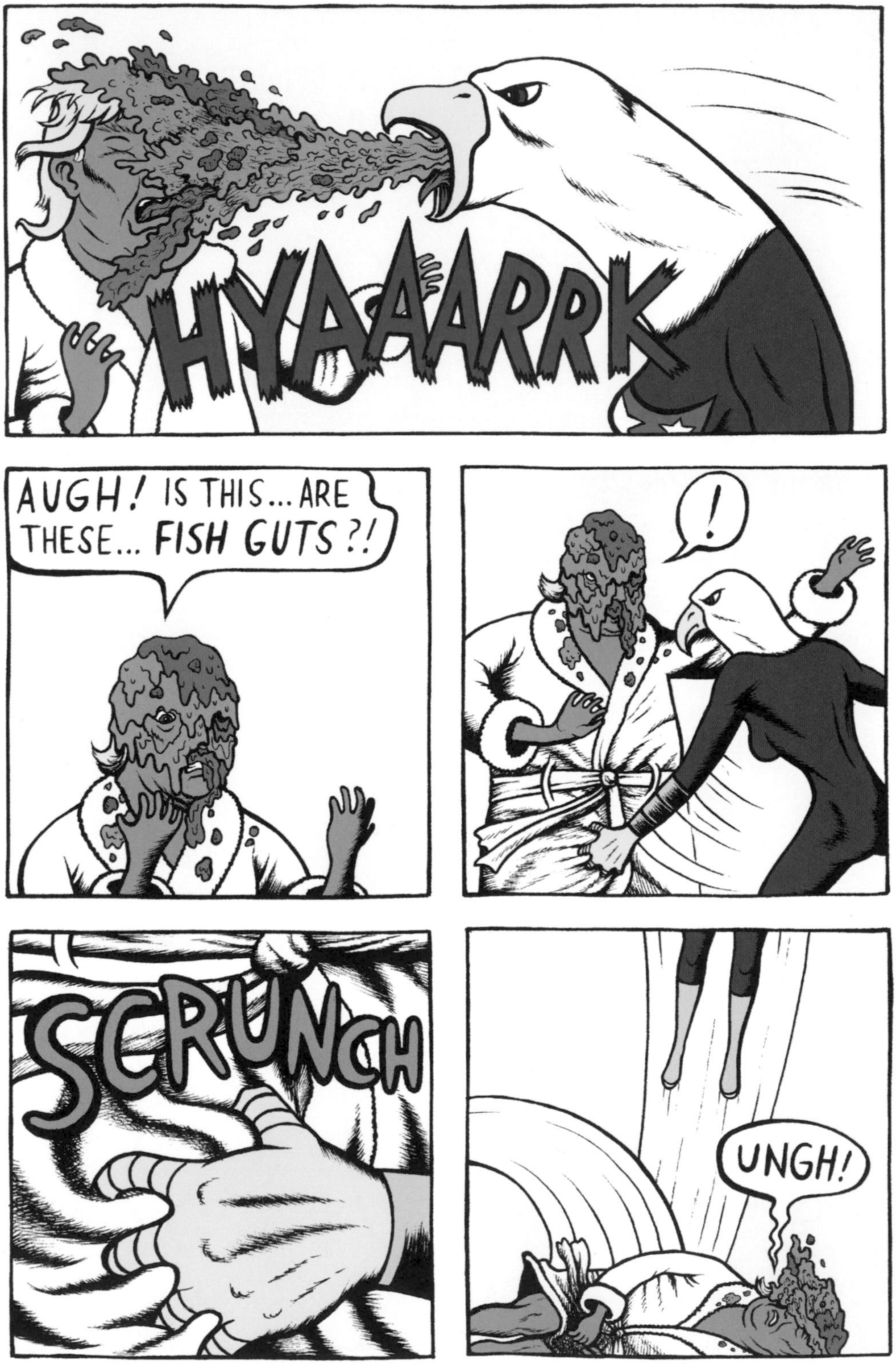
HYAARRK
AUGH! IS THIS... ARE THESE... FISH GUTS?!
!
SCRUNCH
UNGH!

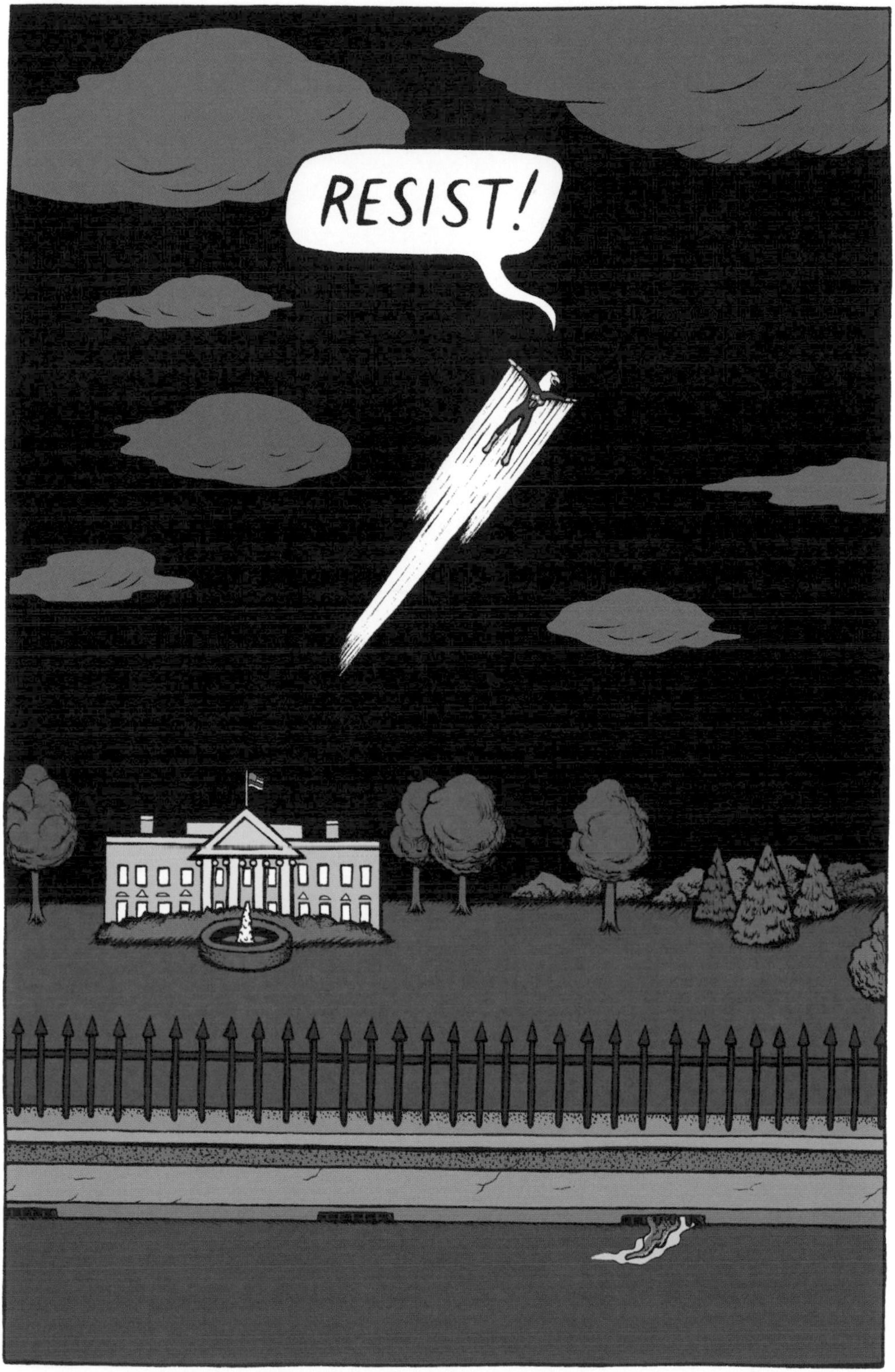
RESIST!

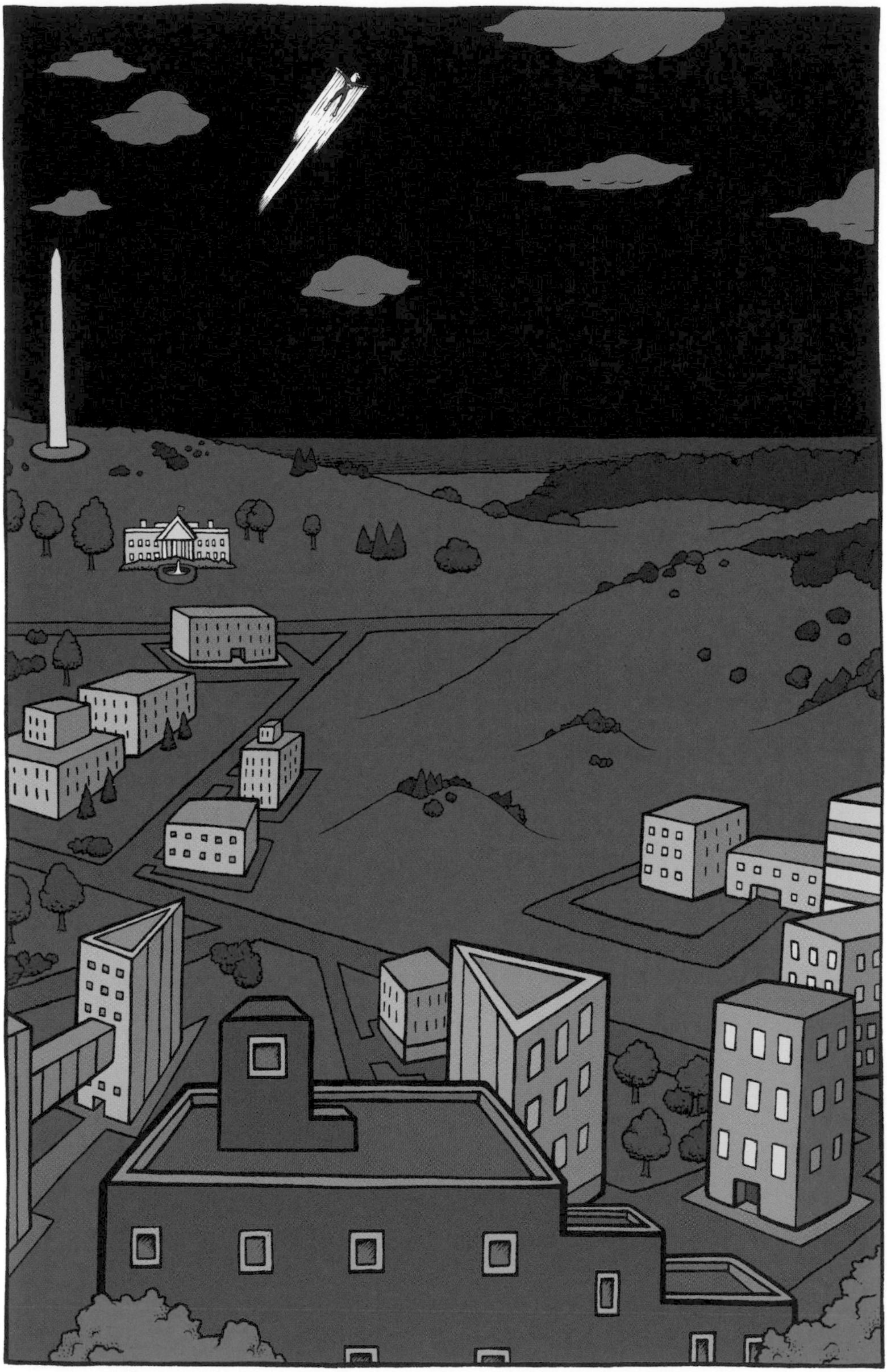

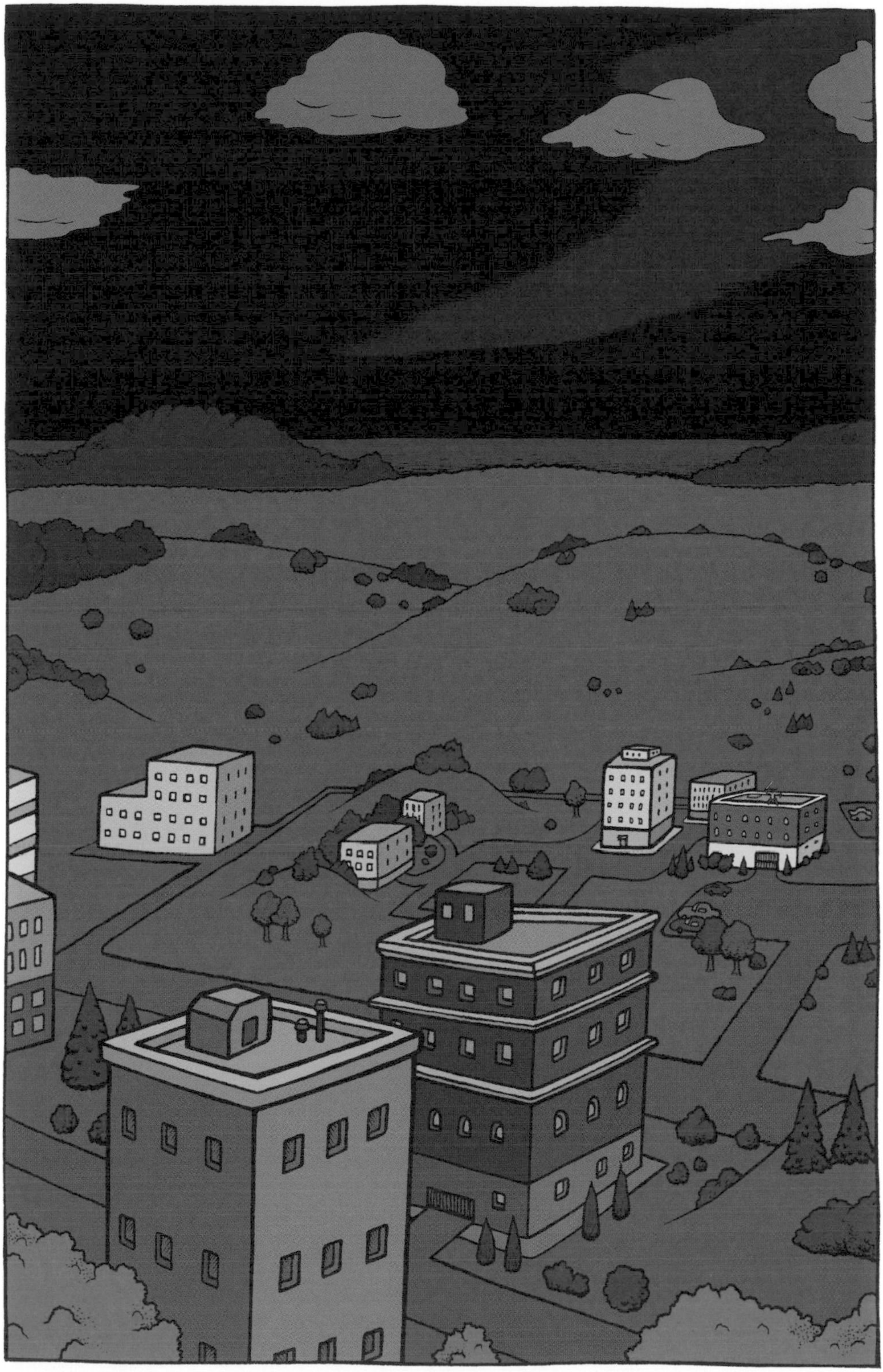

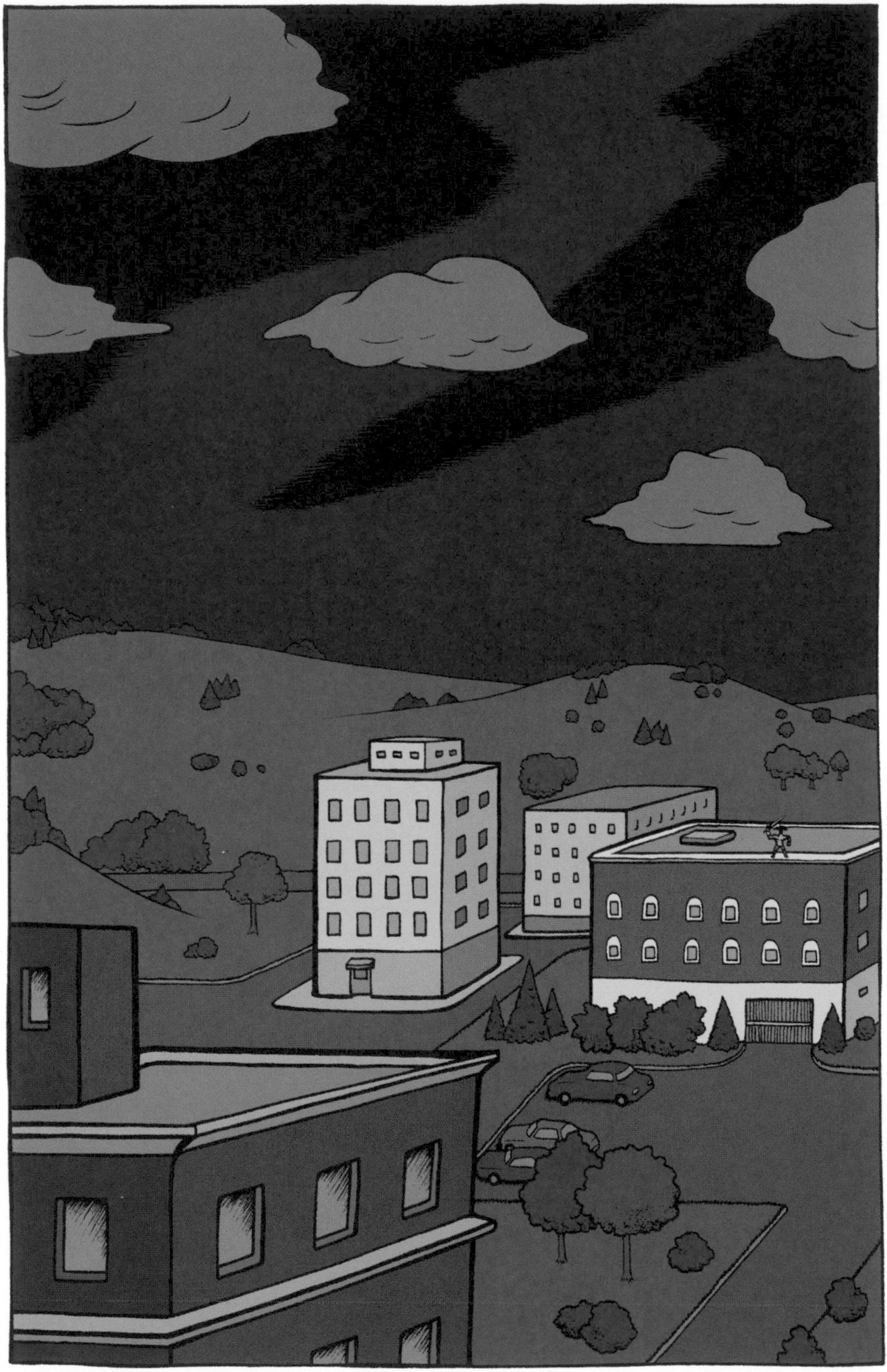

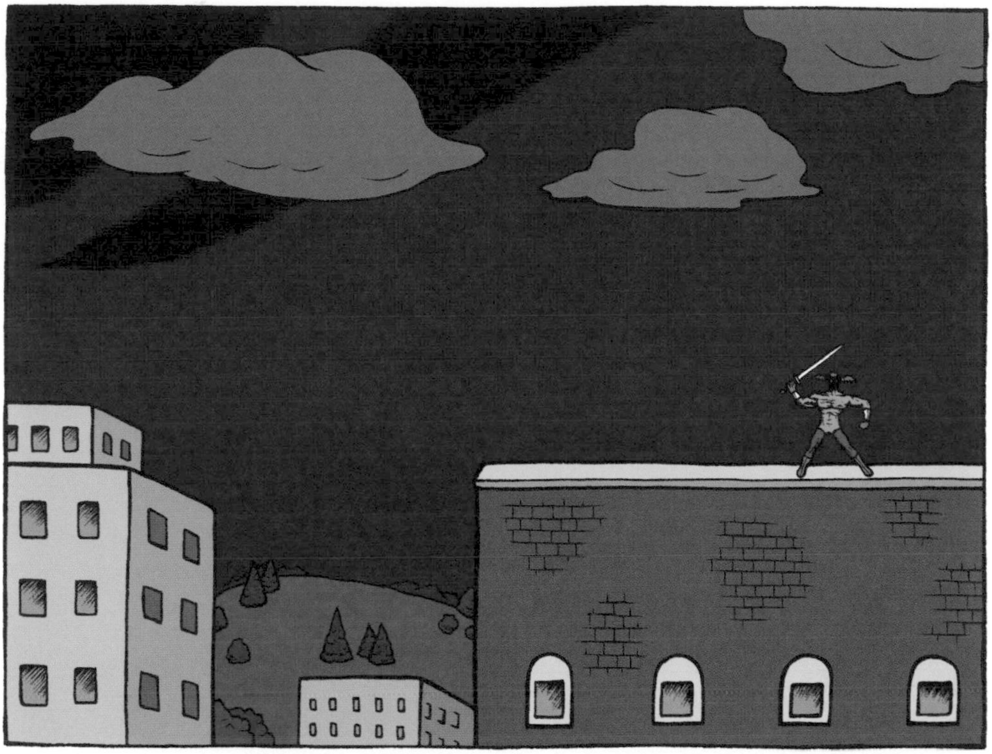

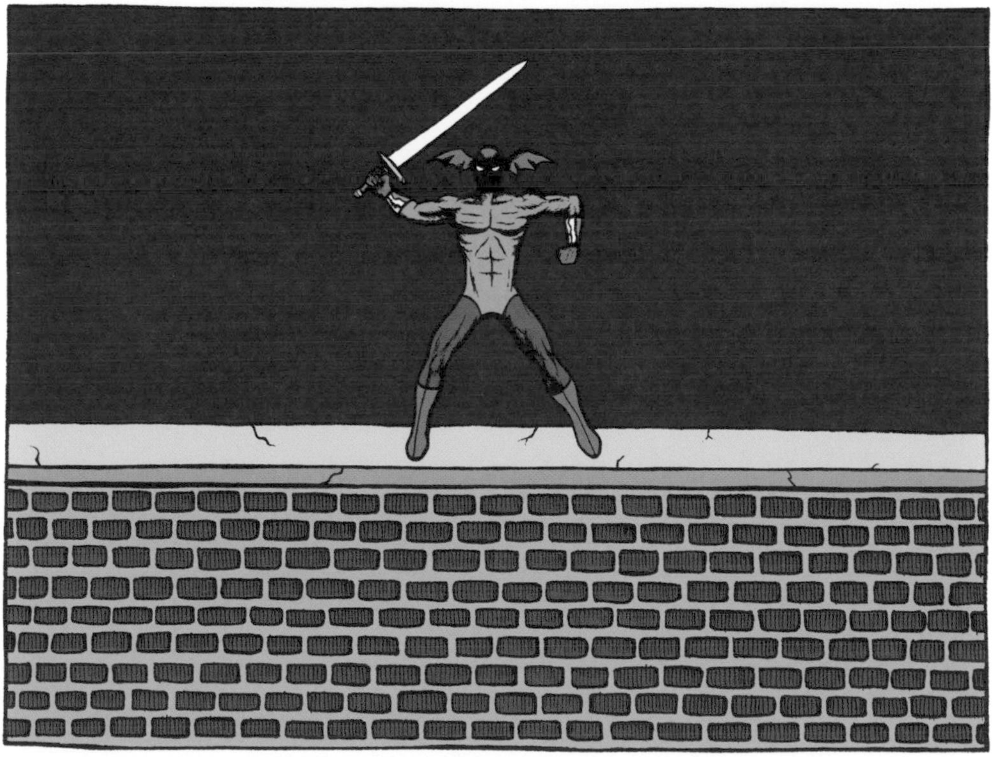

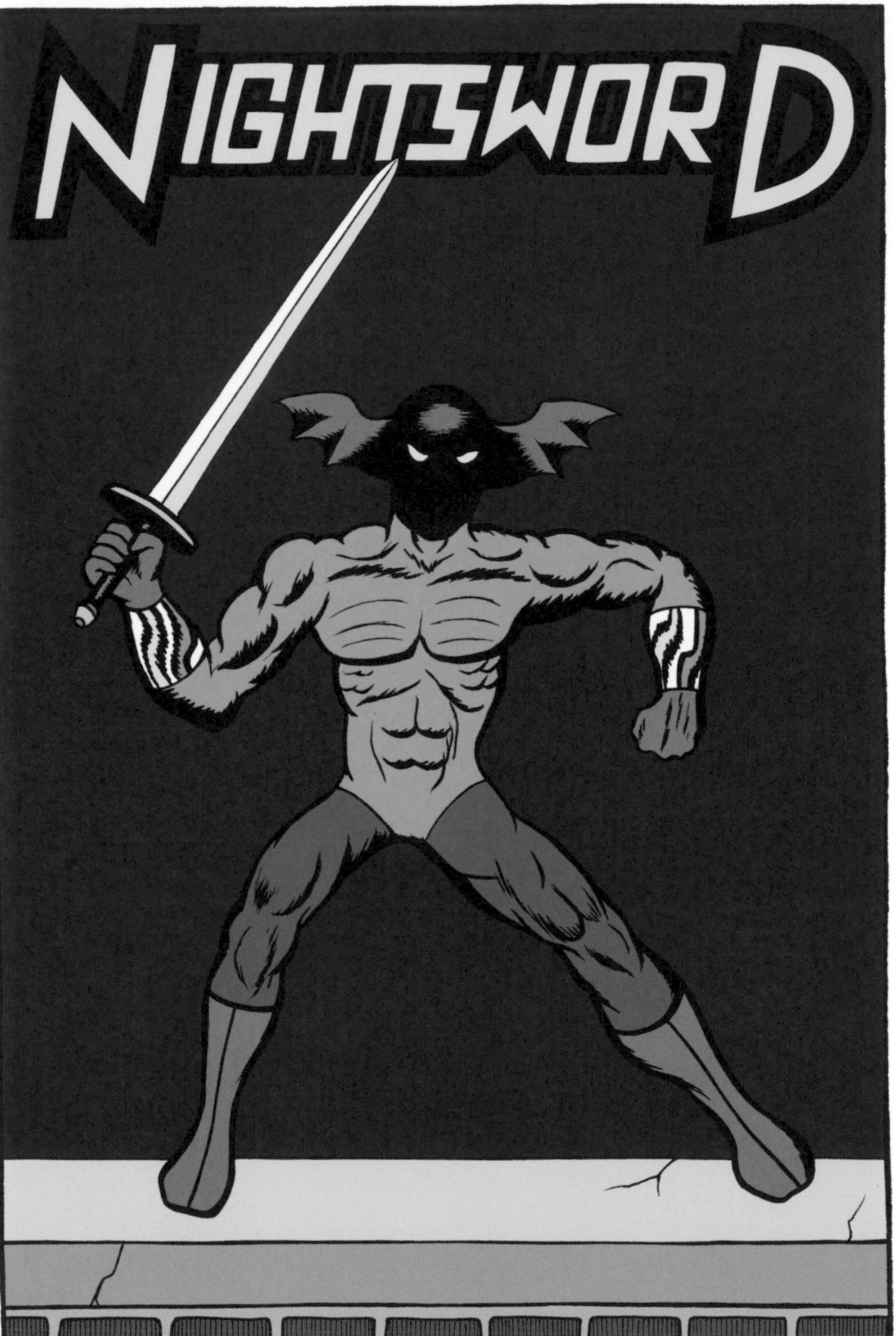
NIGHTSWORD

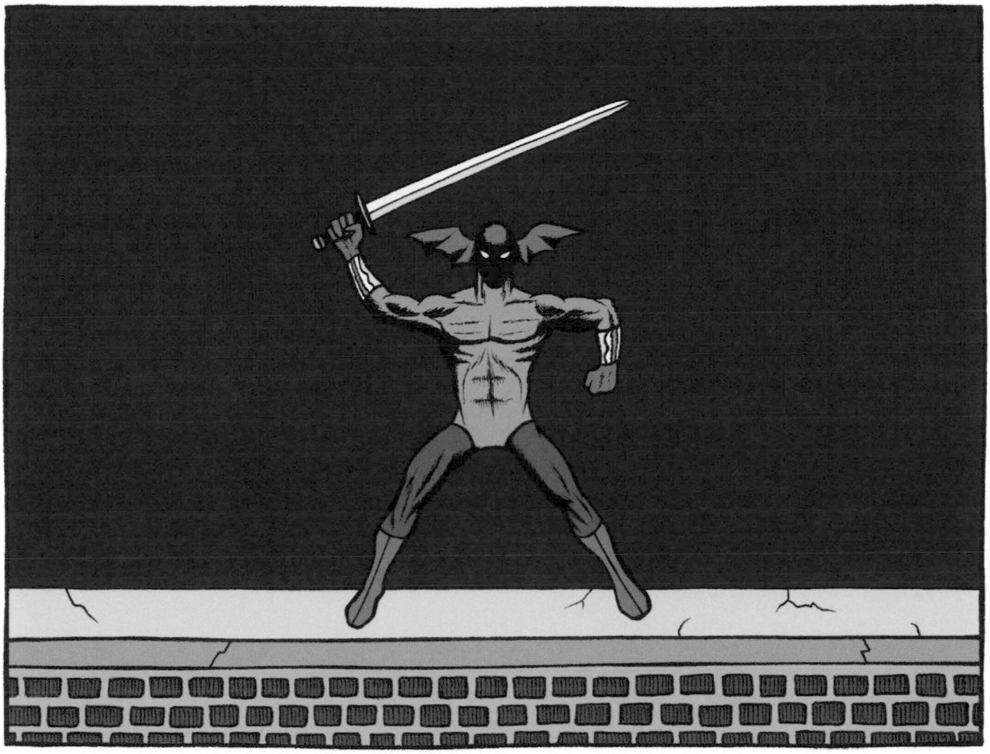

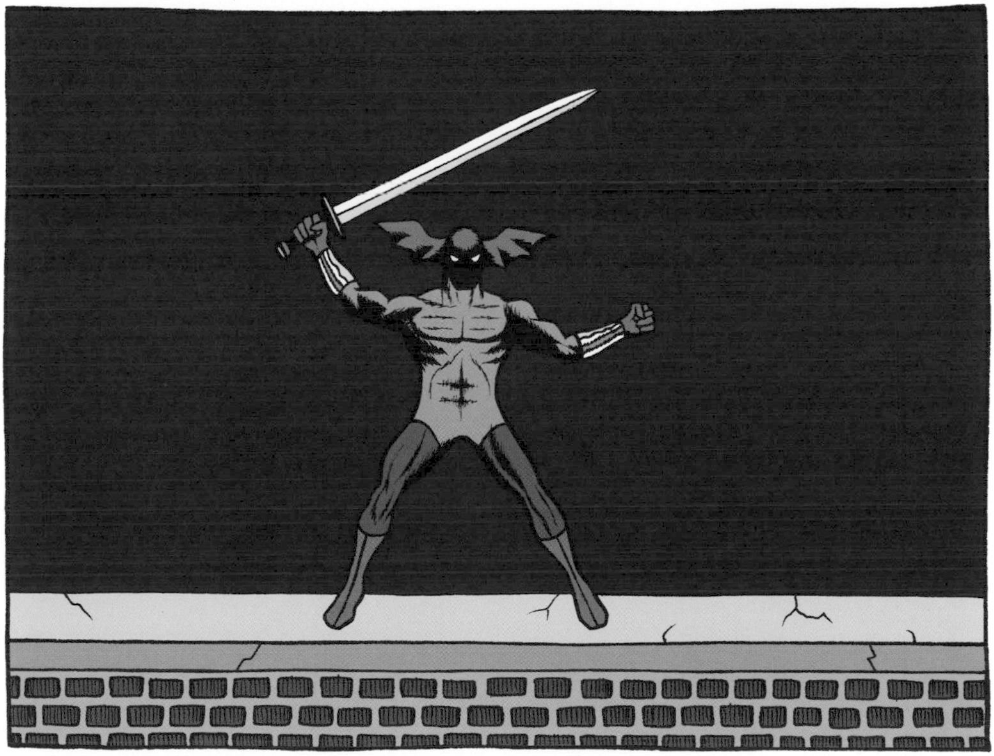

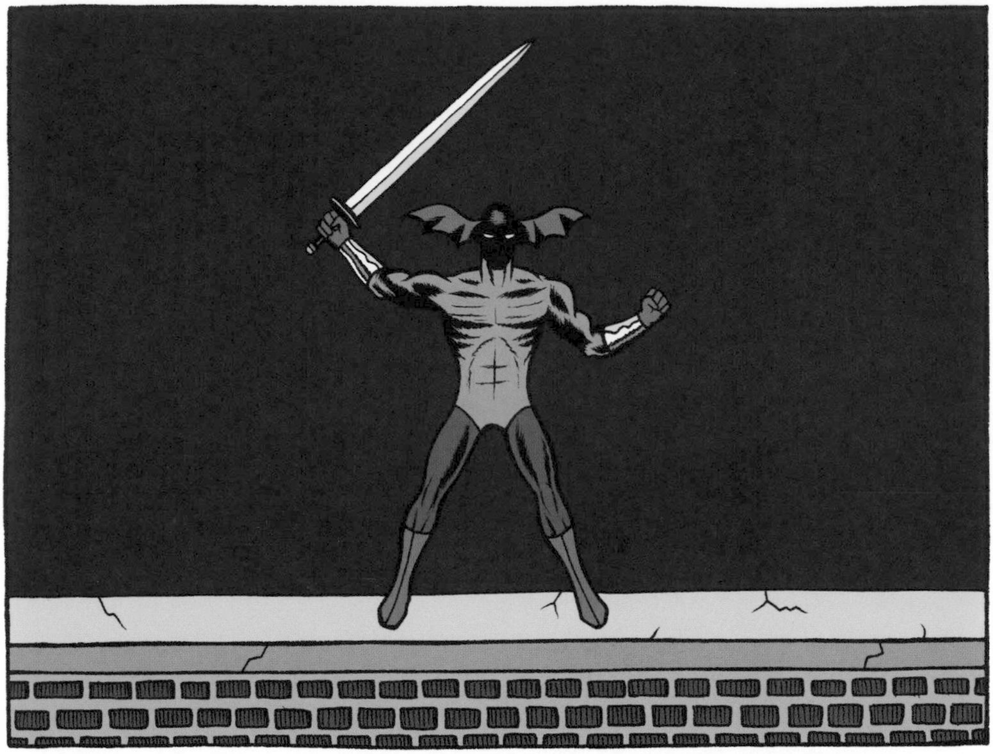

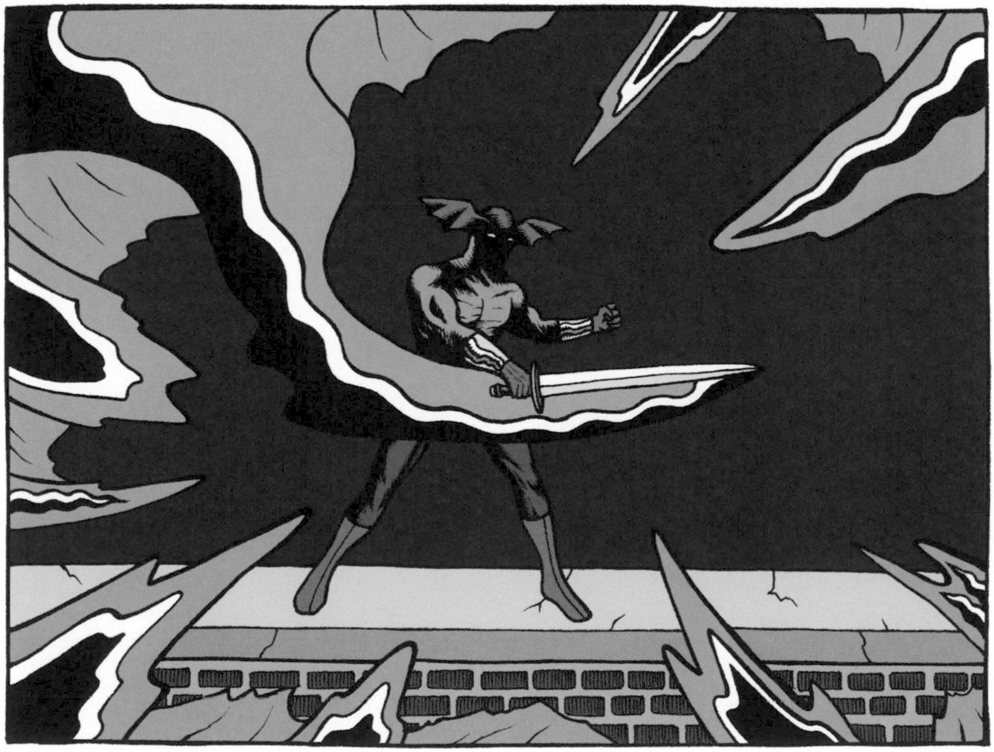

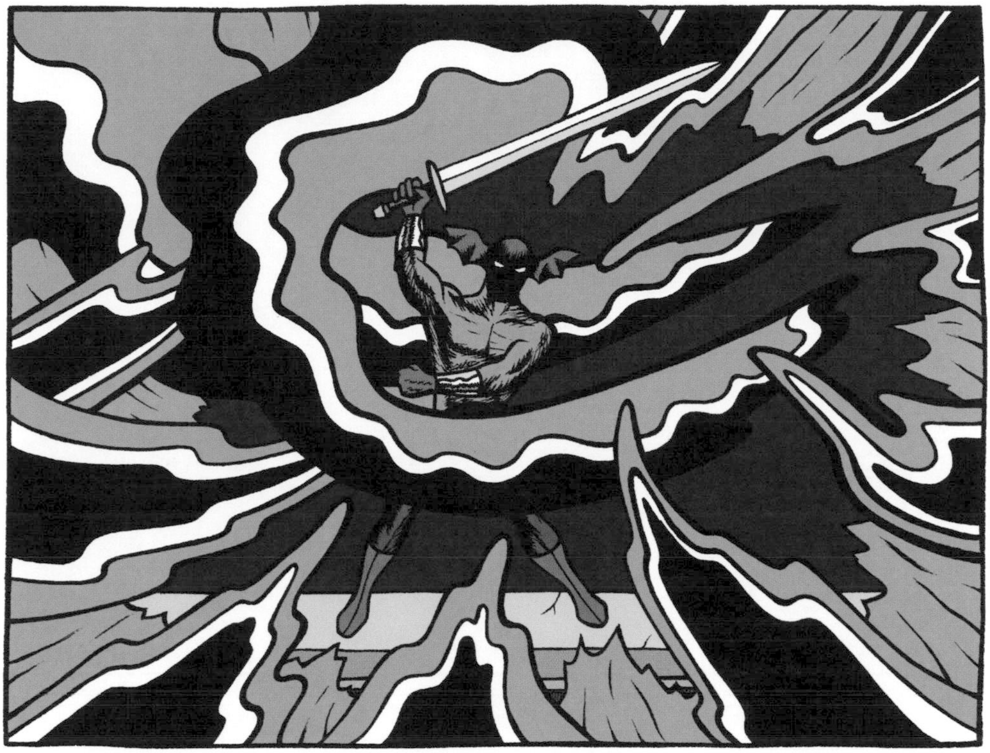

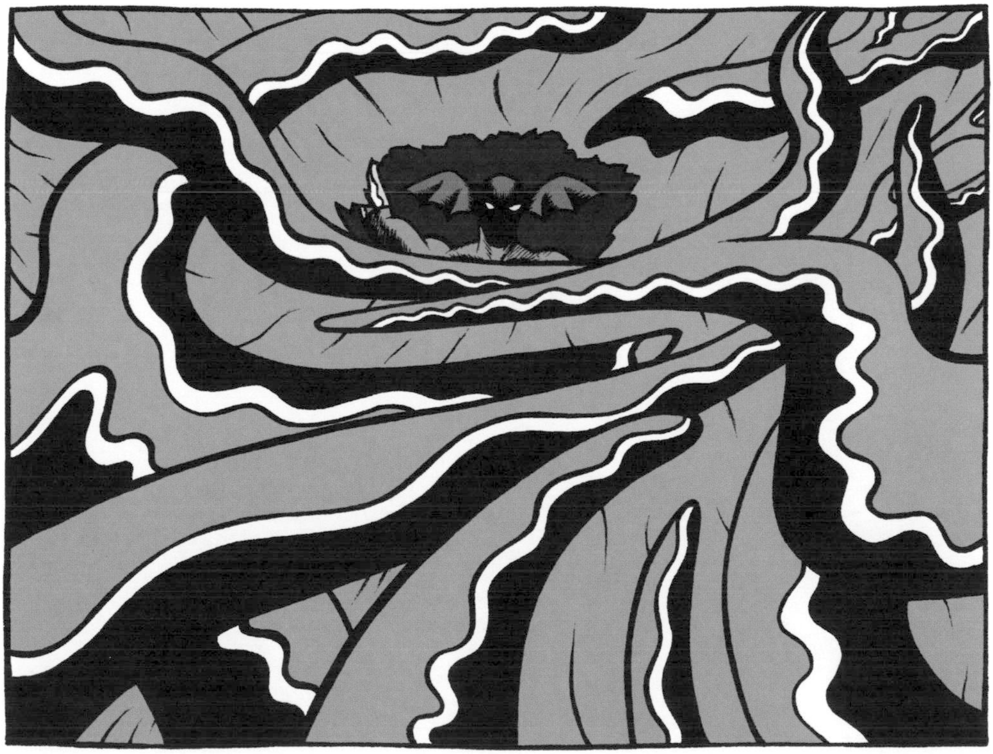

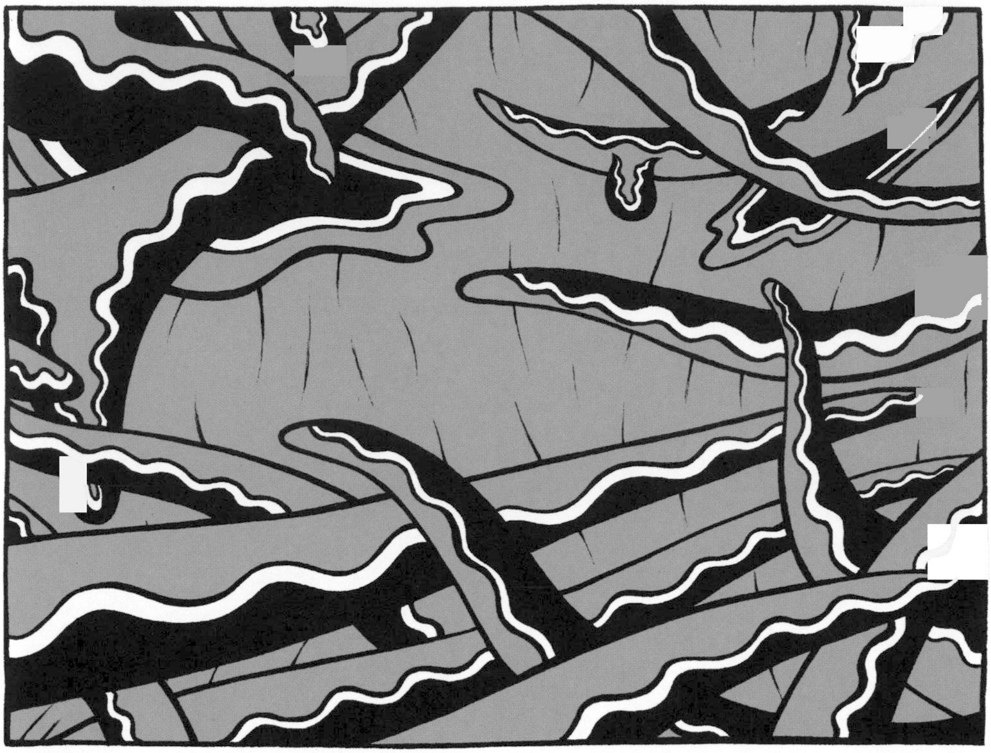

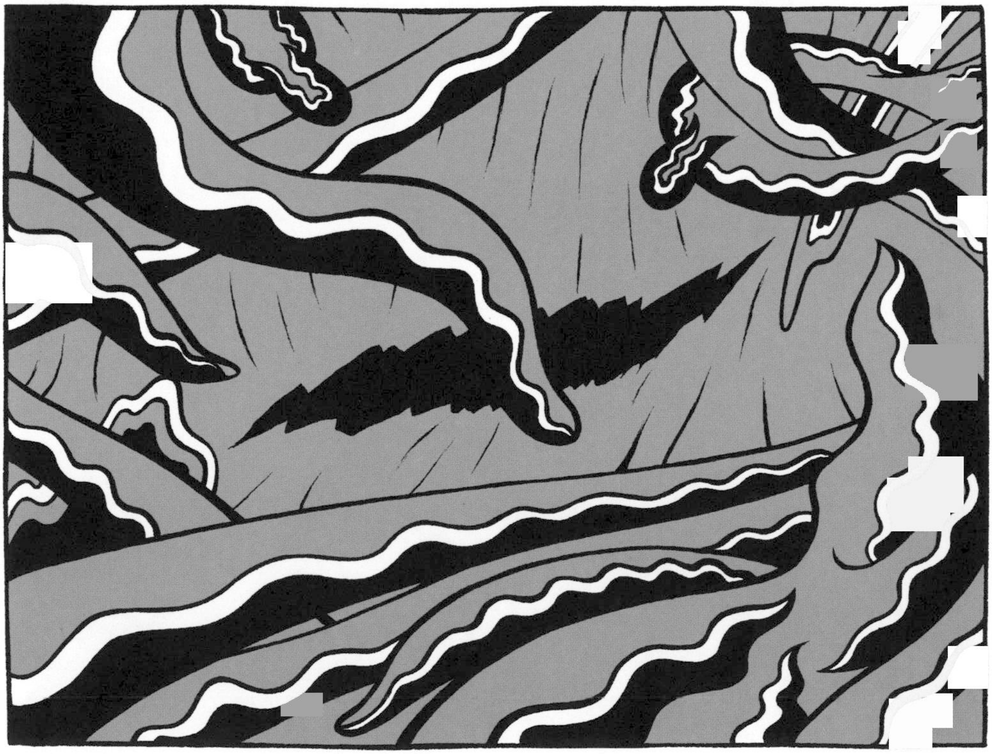

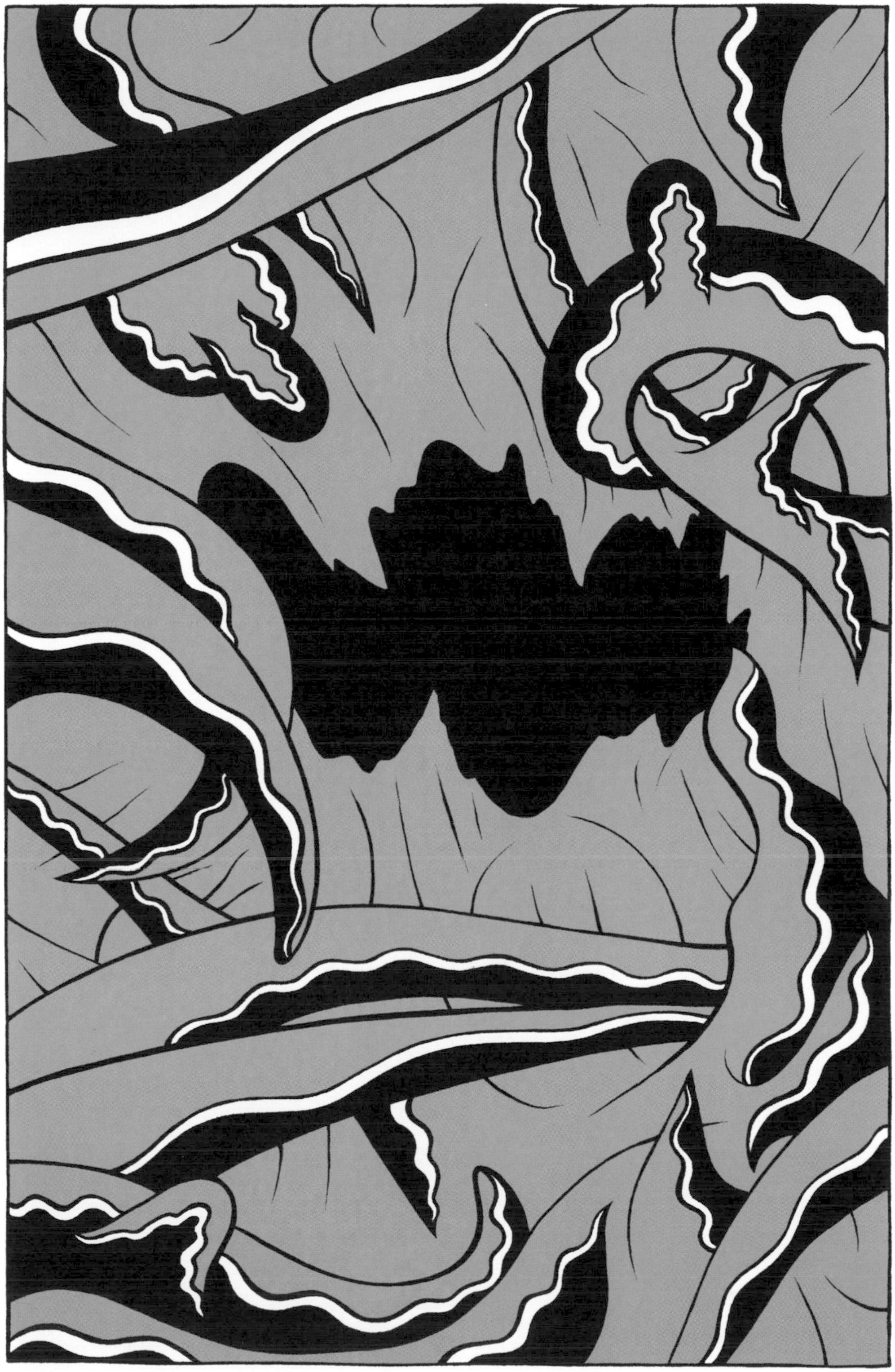

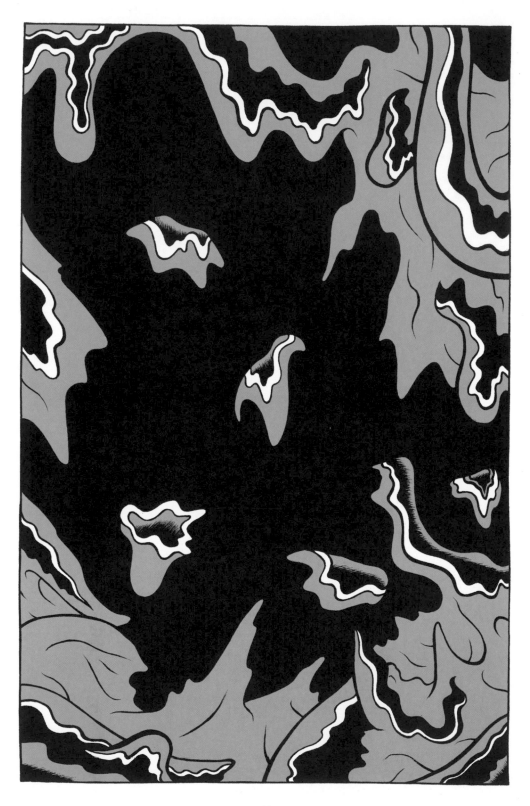

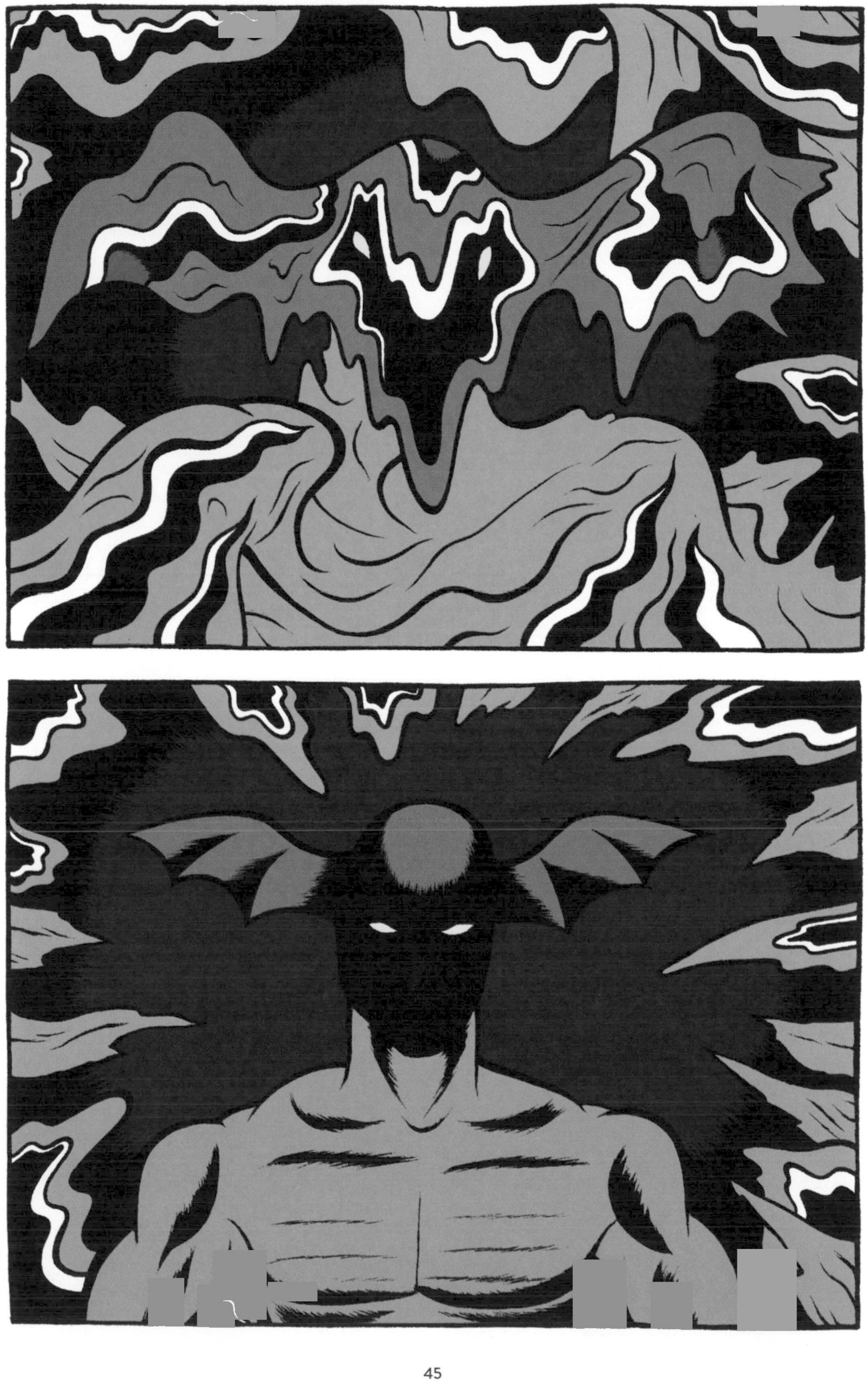

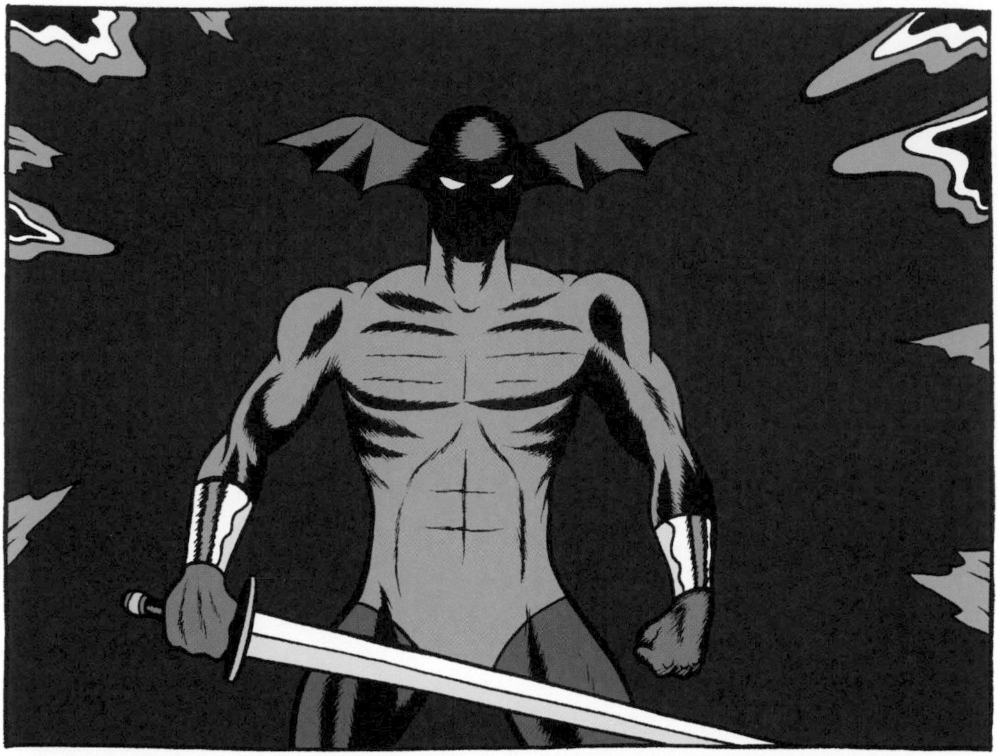

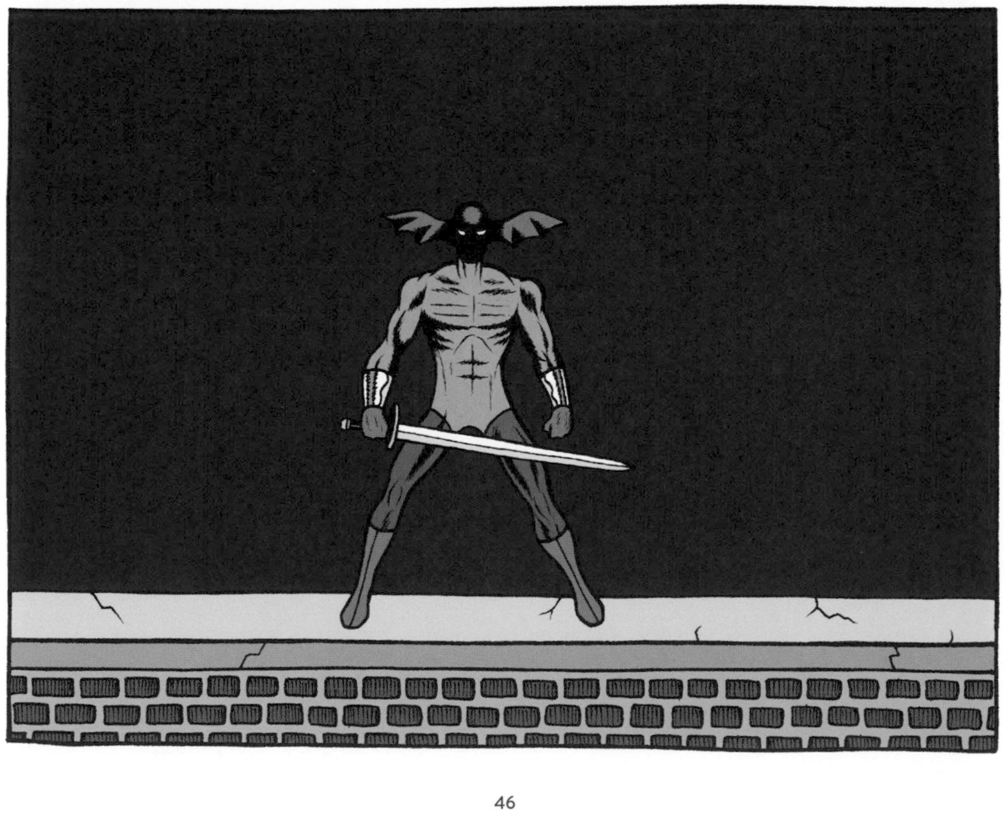

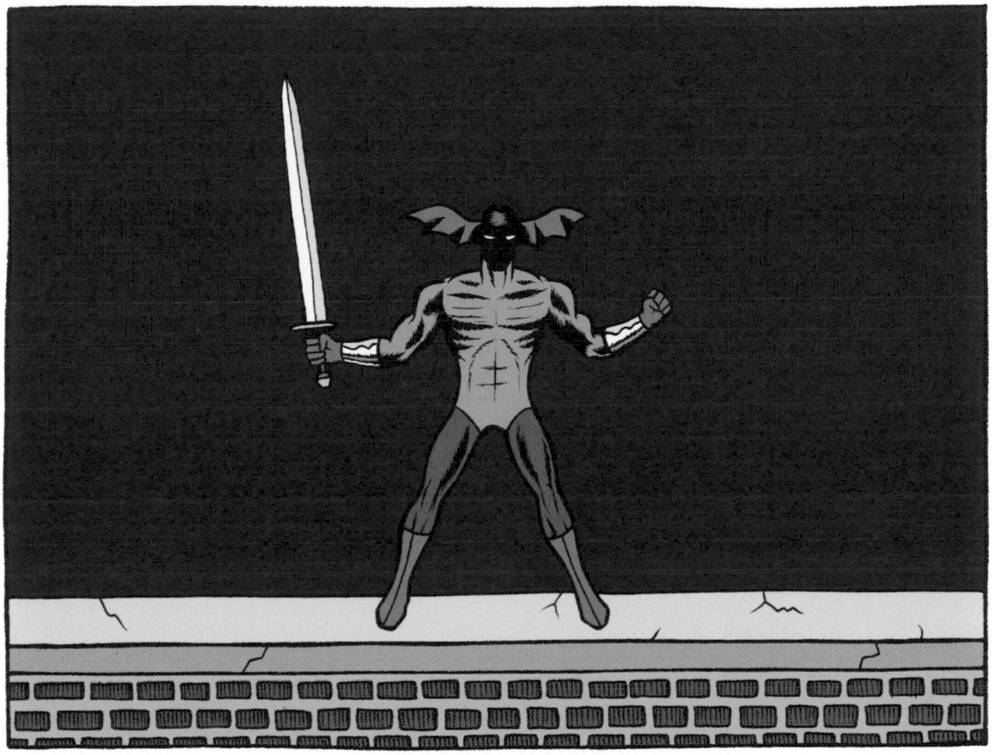

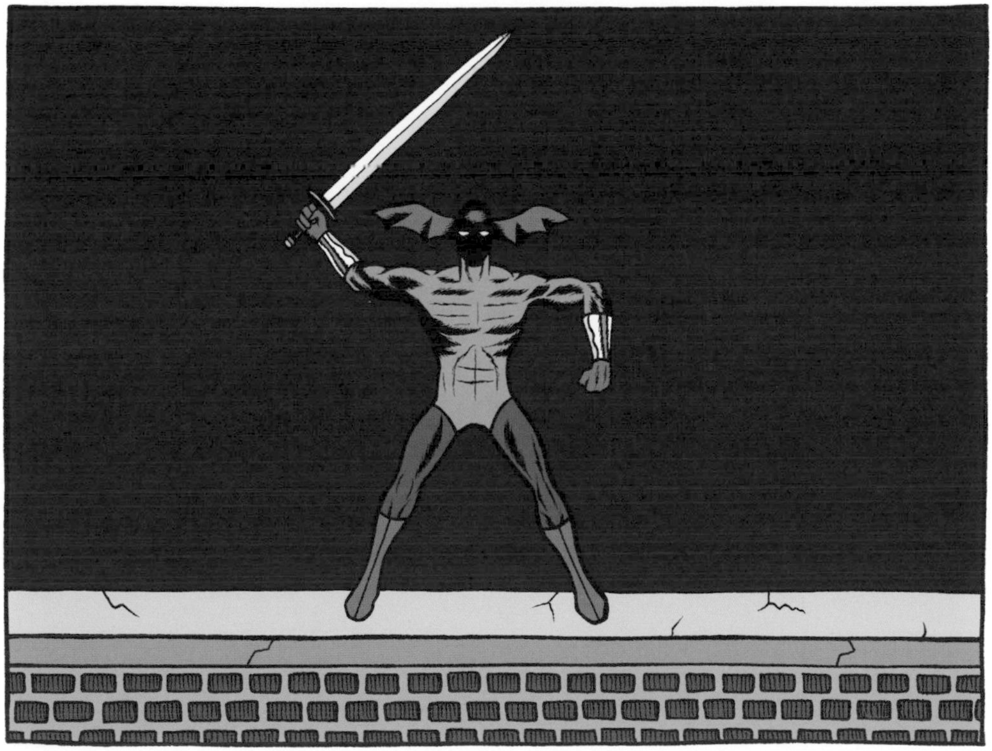

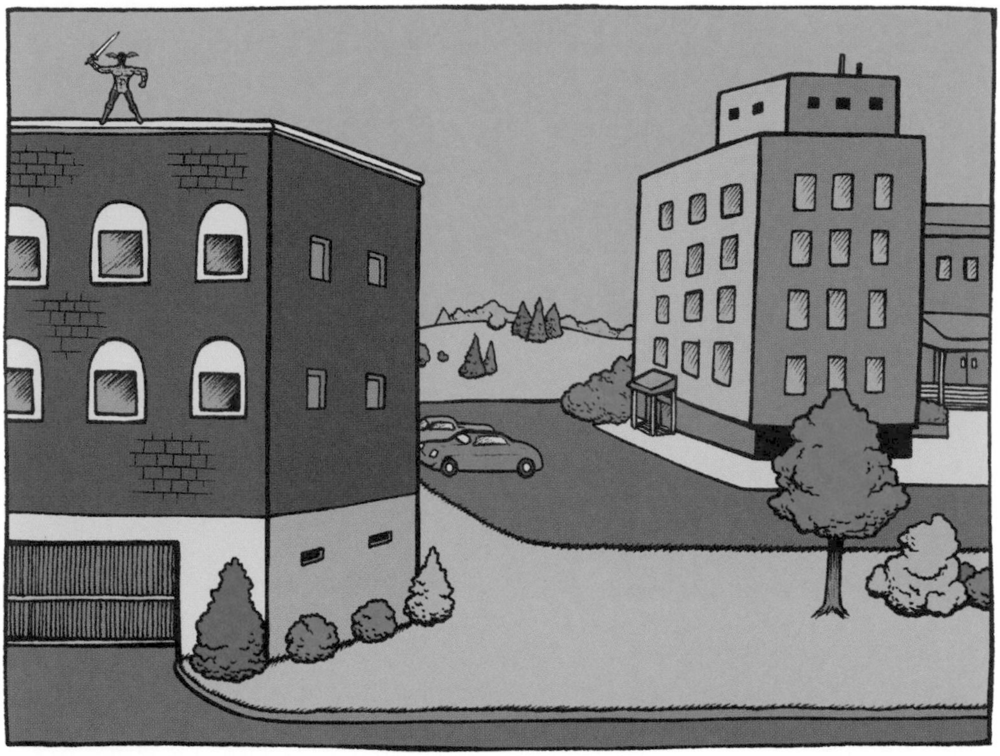

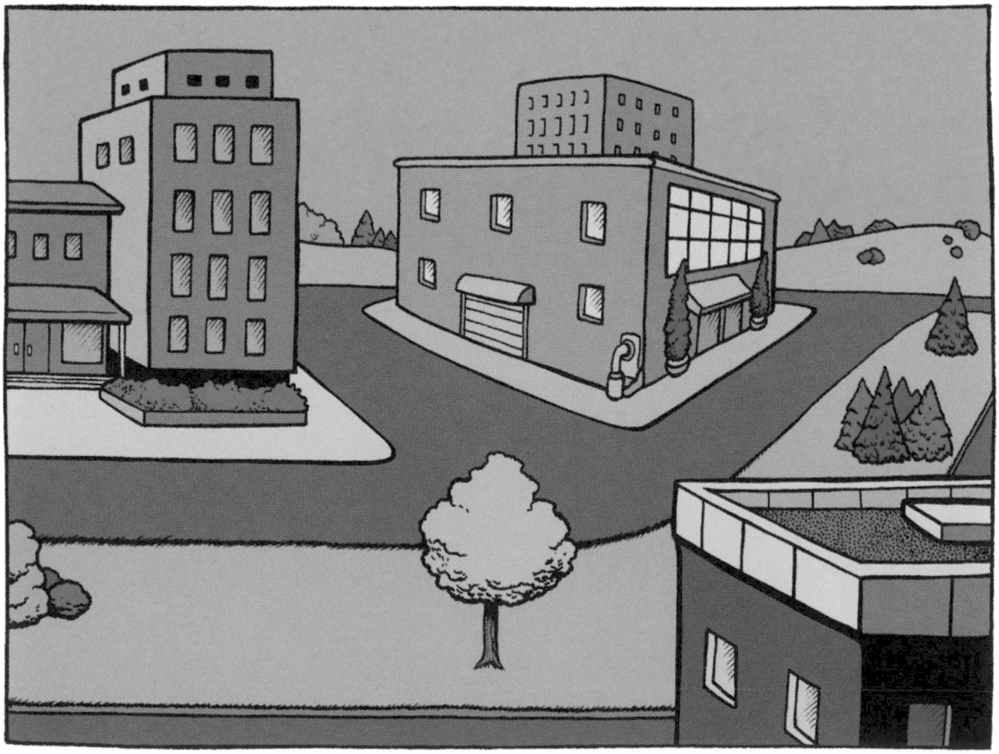

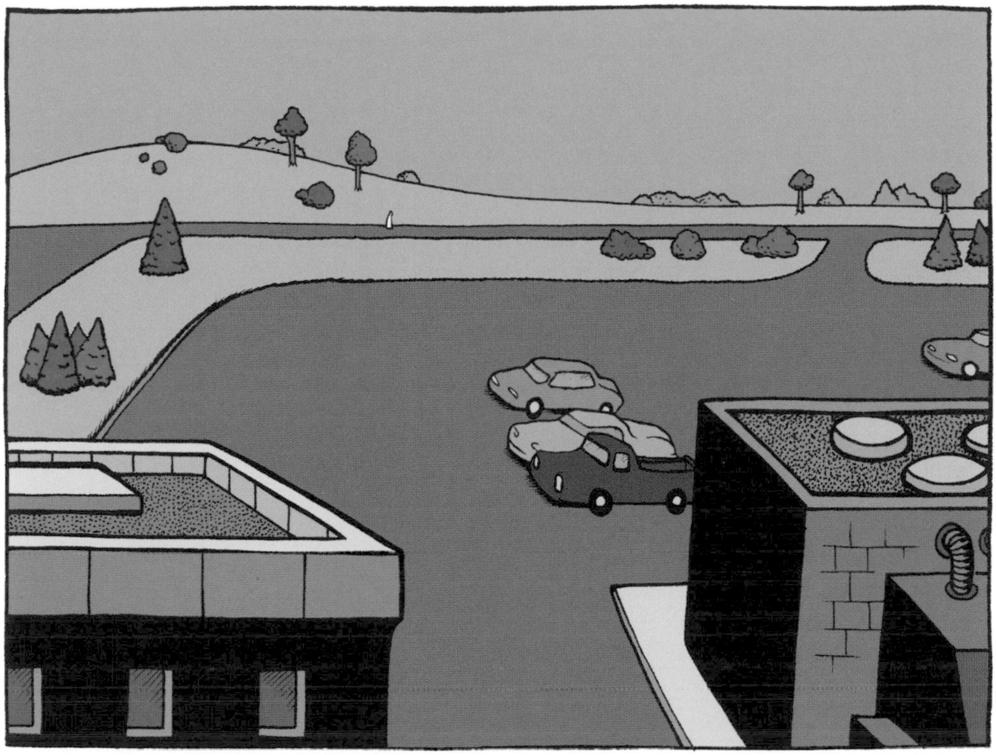

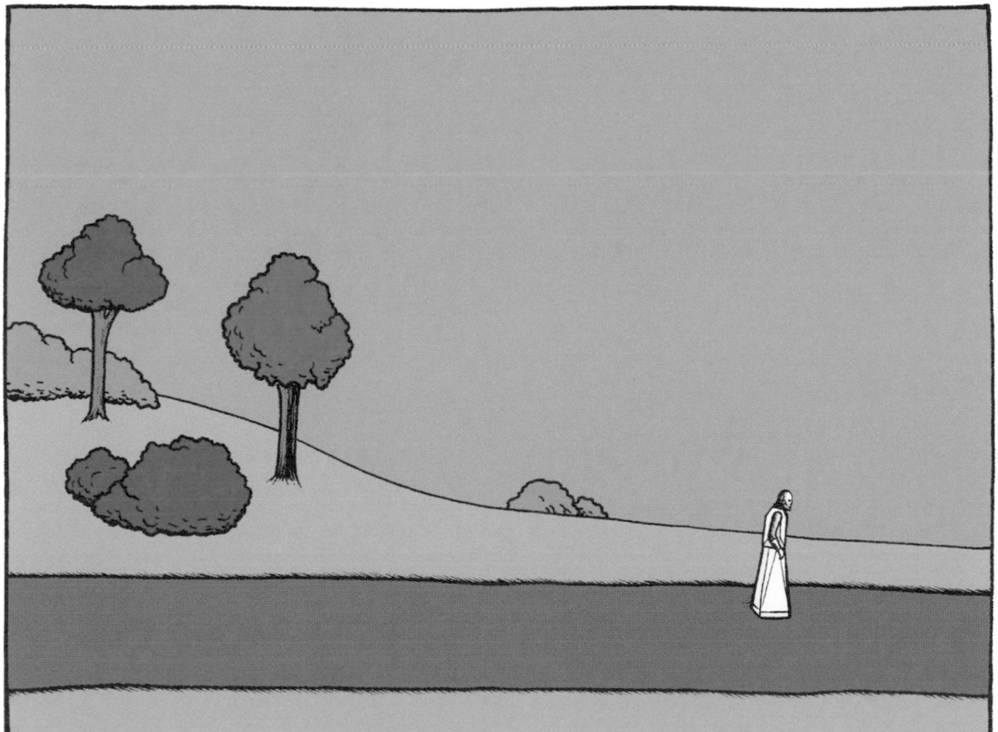

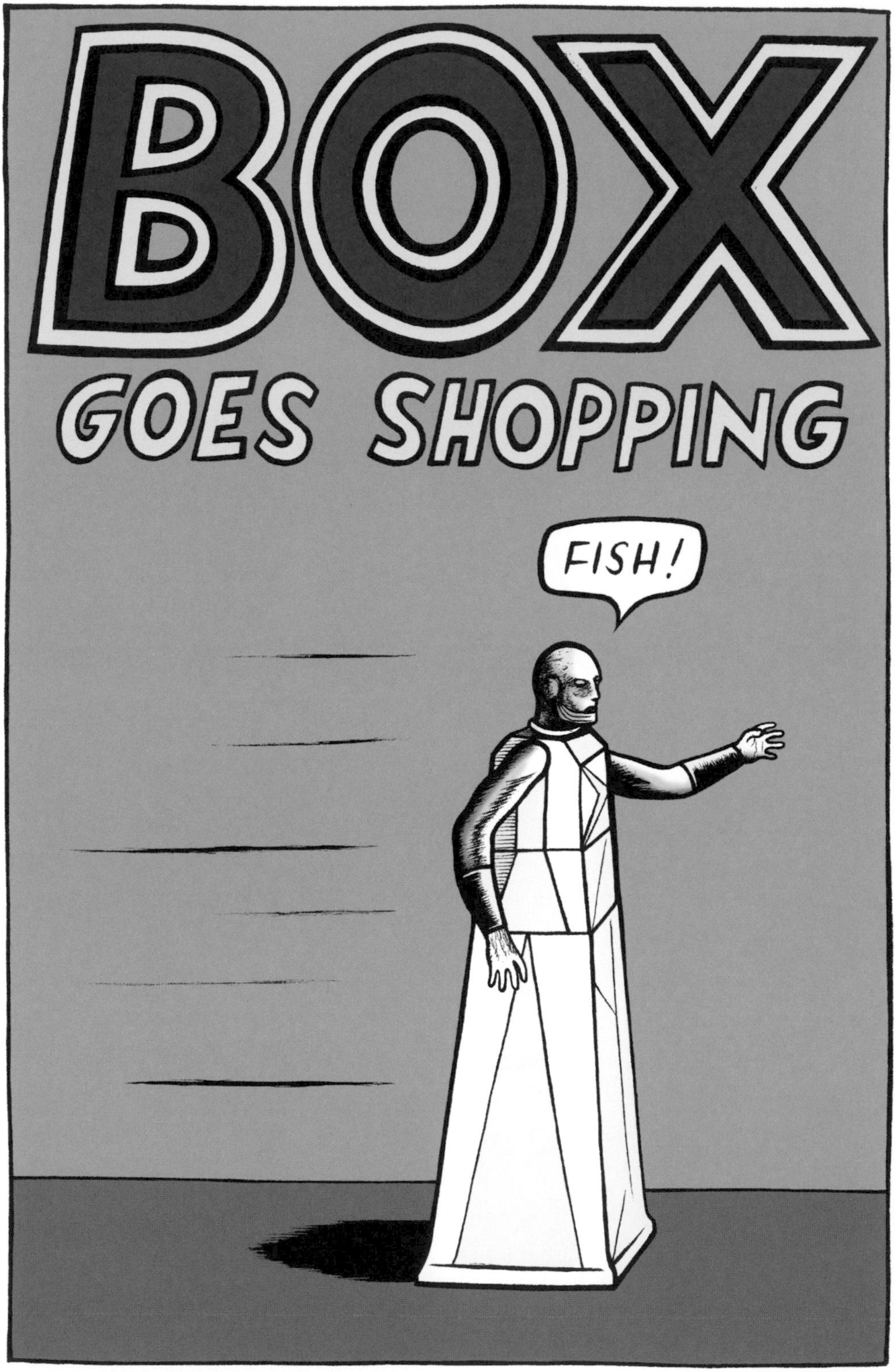
BOX
GOES SHOPPING
FISH!

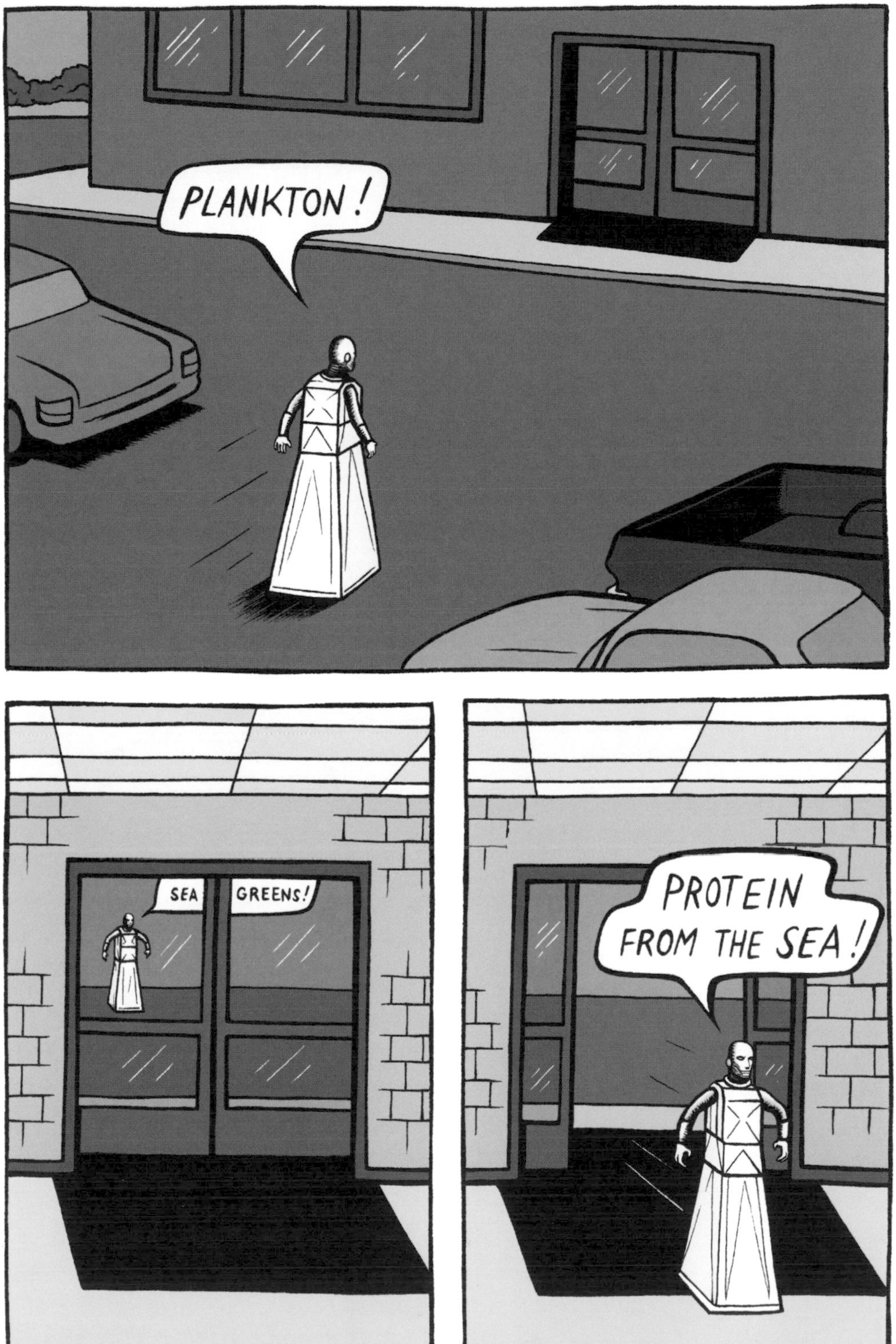
PLANKTON!
SEA
GREENS!
PROTEIN FROM THE SEA!

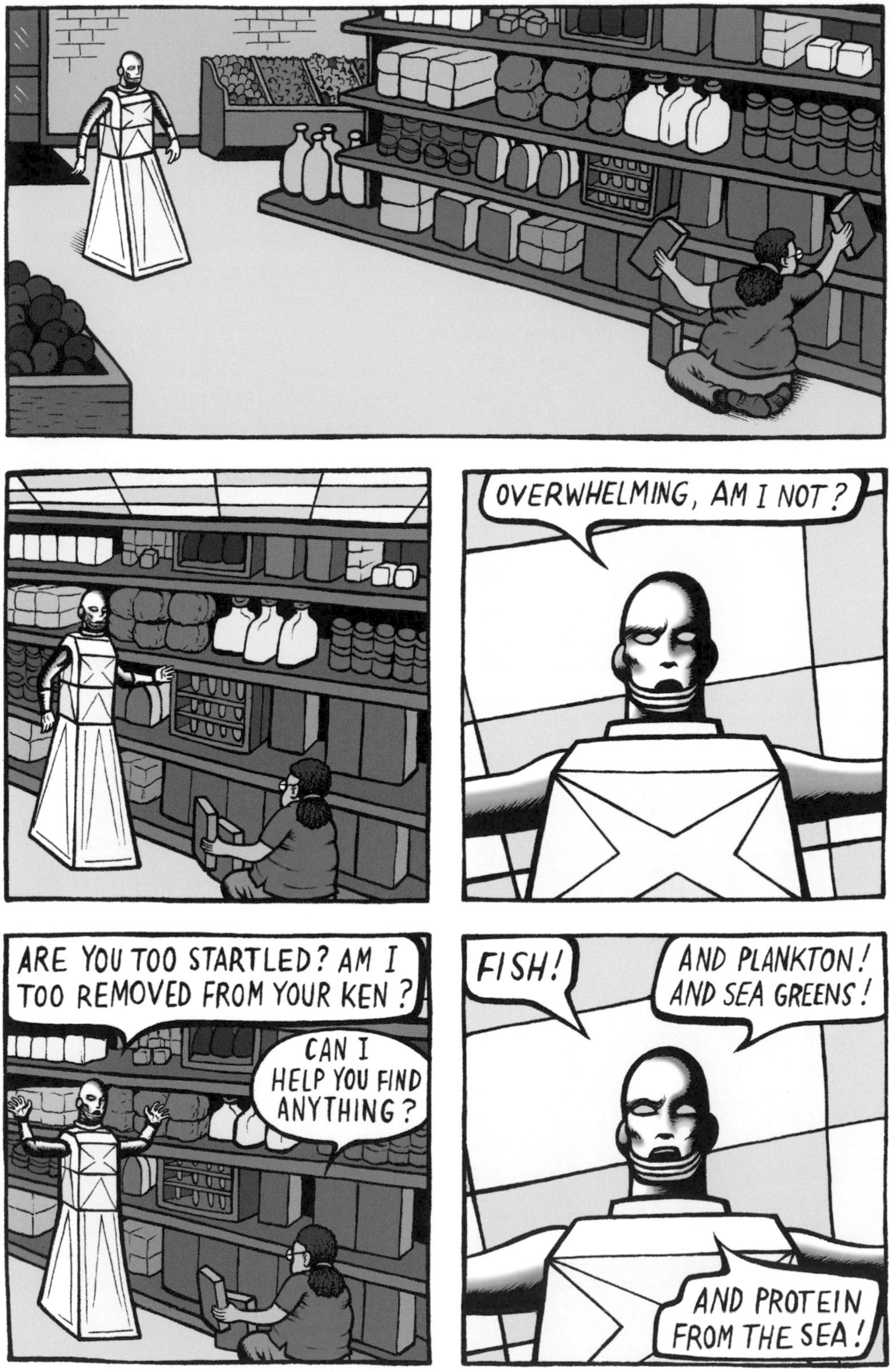
OVERWHELMING, AM I NOT?
ARE YOU TOO STARTLED? AM I TOO REMOVED FROM YOUR KEN?
CAN I HELP YOU FIND ANYTHING?
FISH!
AND PLANKTON! AND SEA GREENS!
AND PROTEIN FROM THE SEA!

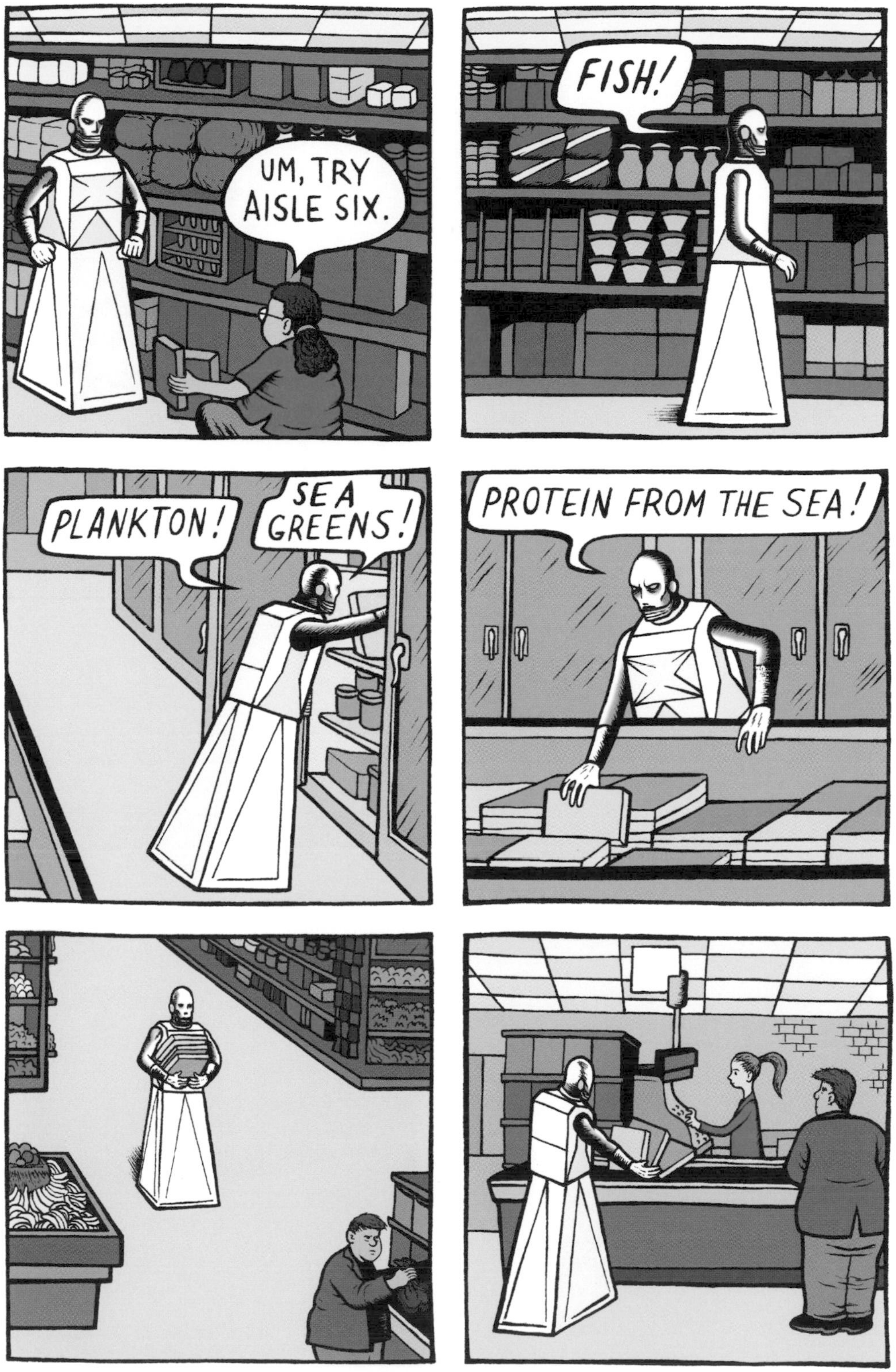
UM, TRY AISLE SIX.
FISH!
PLANKTON!
SEA GREENS!
PROTEIN FROM THE SEA!

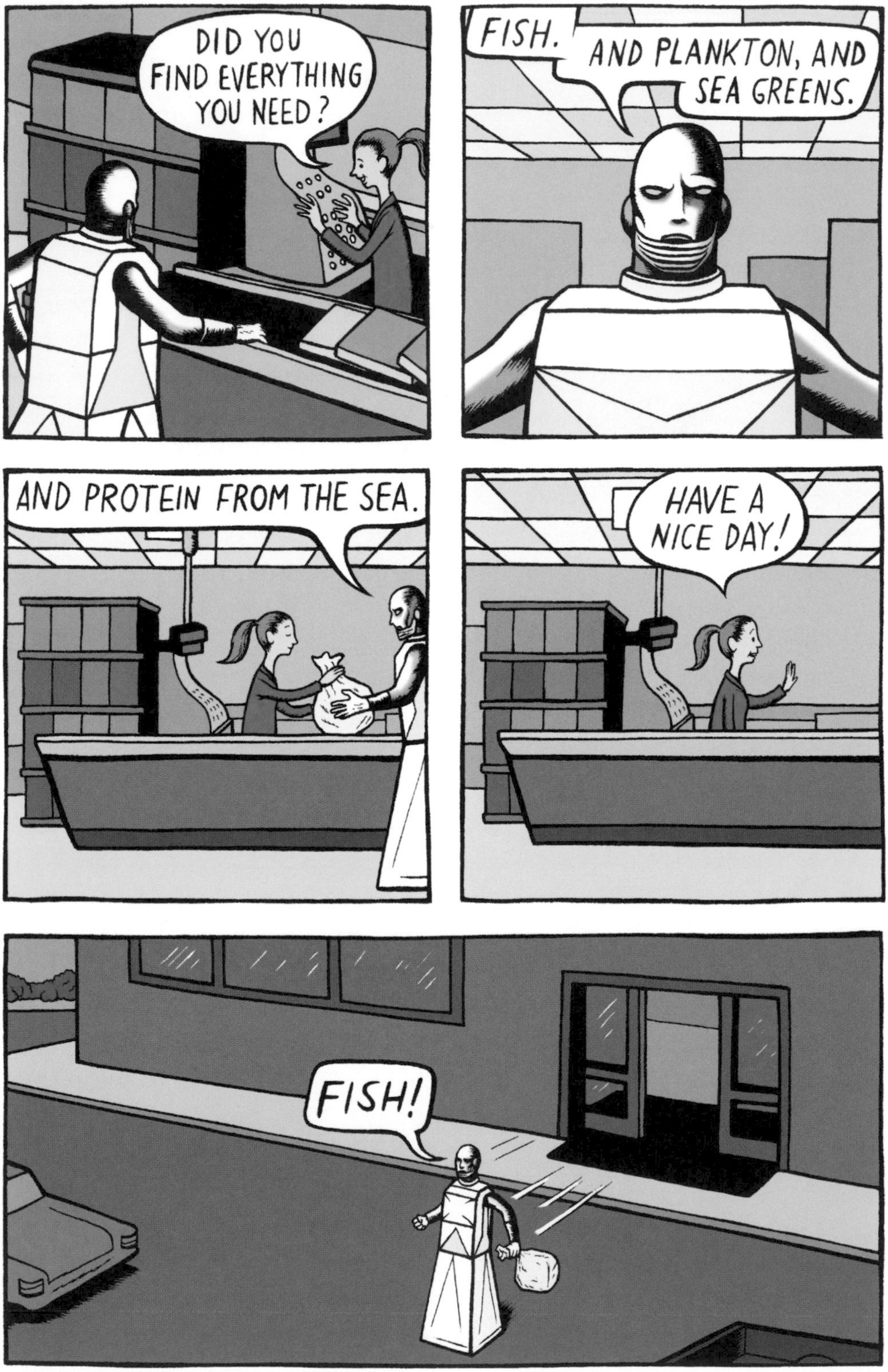
DID YOU FIND EVERYTHING YOU NEED?
FISH.
AND PLANKTON, AND SEA GREENS.
AND PROTEIN FROM THE SEA.
HAVE A NICE DAY!
FISH!

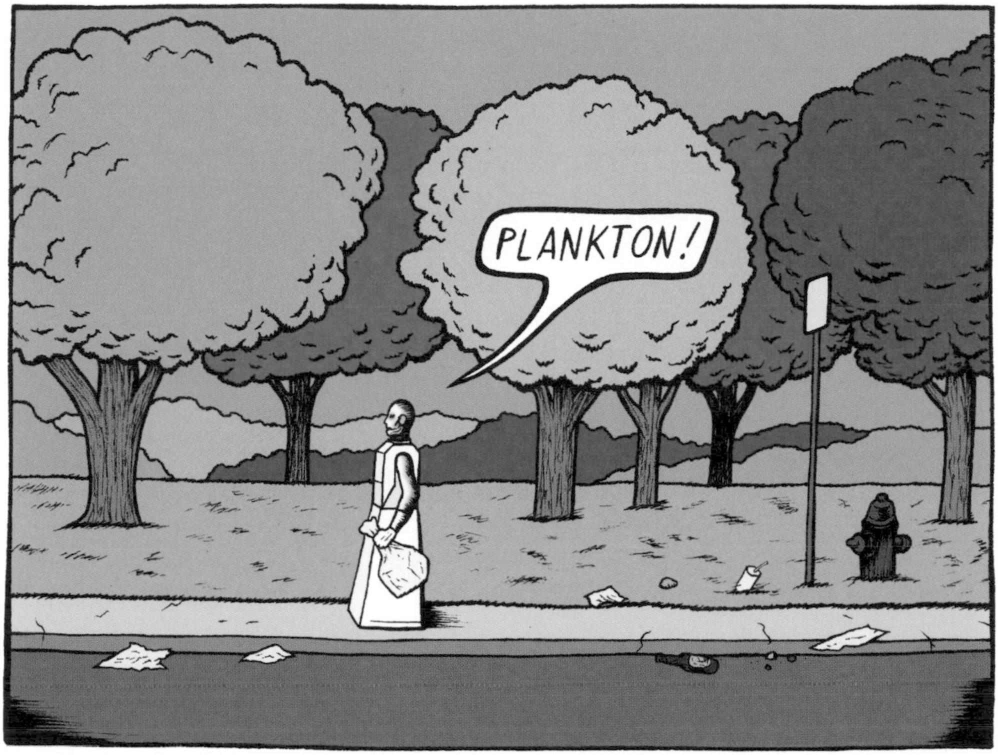
PLANKTON!

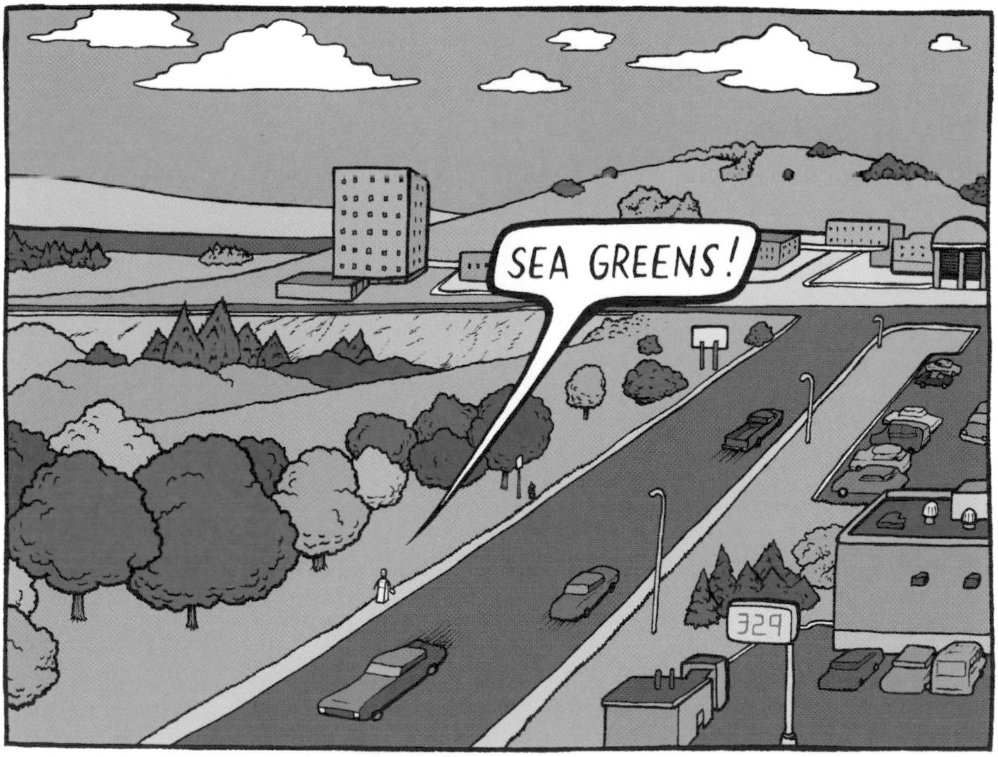
SEA GREENS!
329

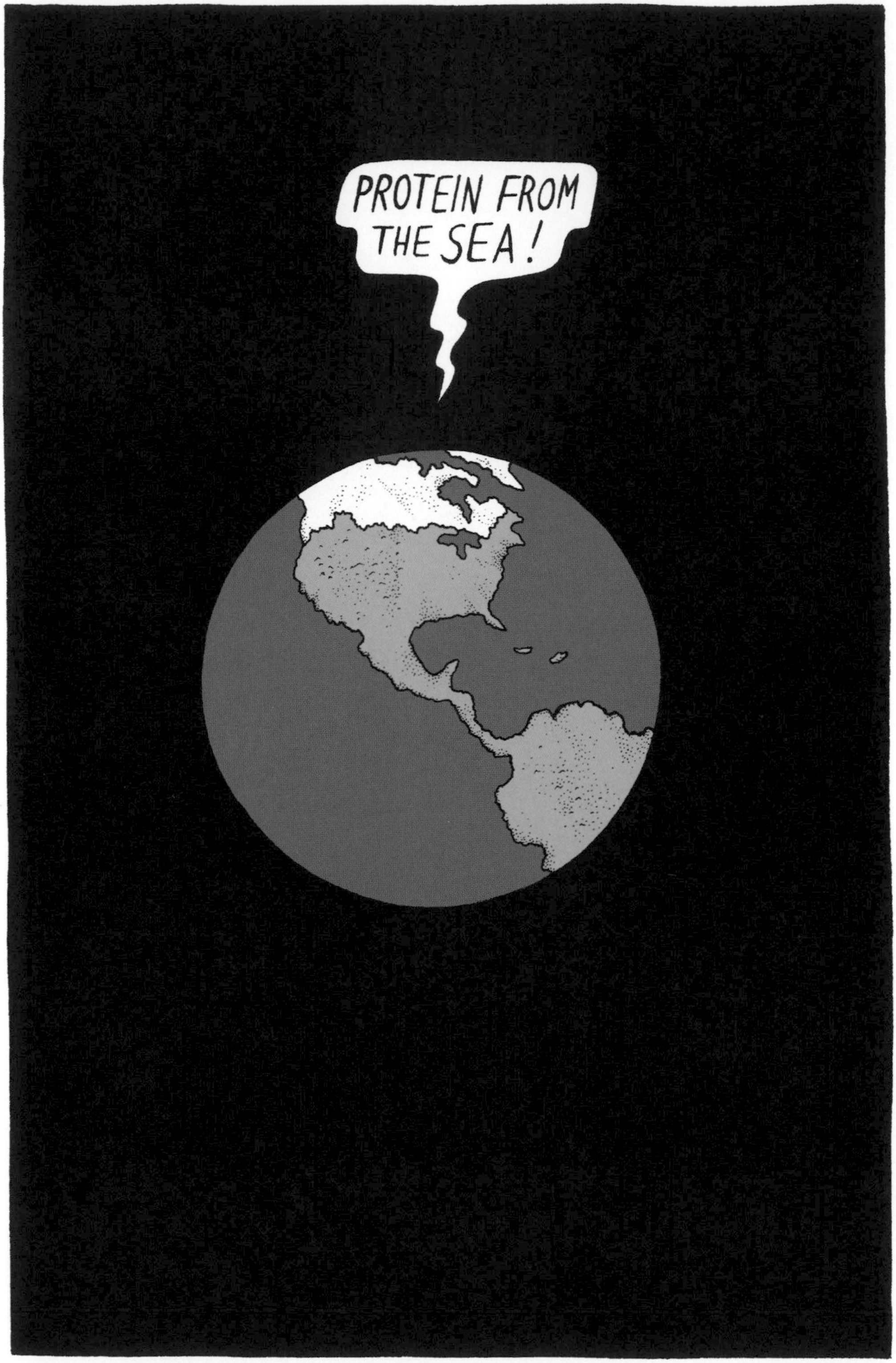
PROTEIN FROM THE SEA!

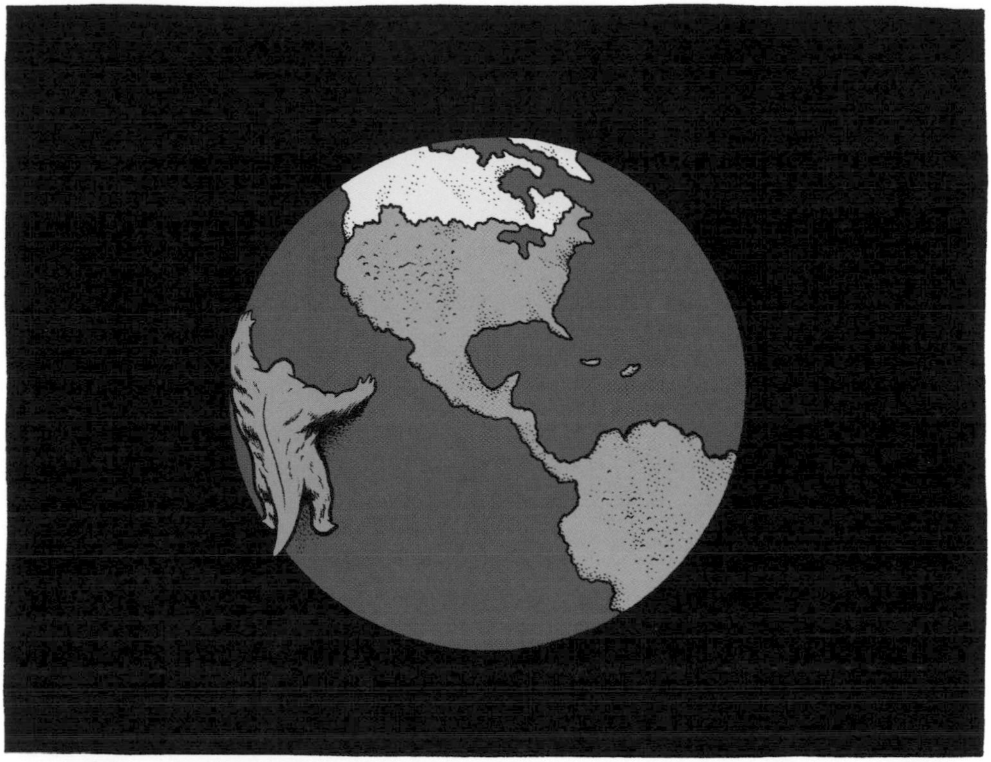

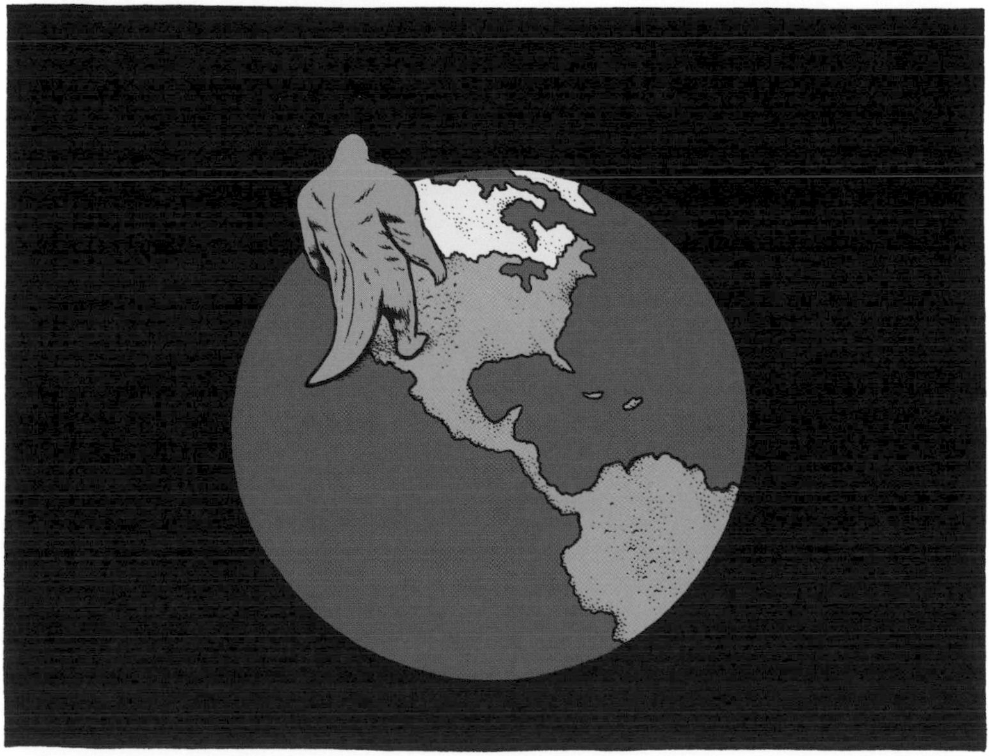

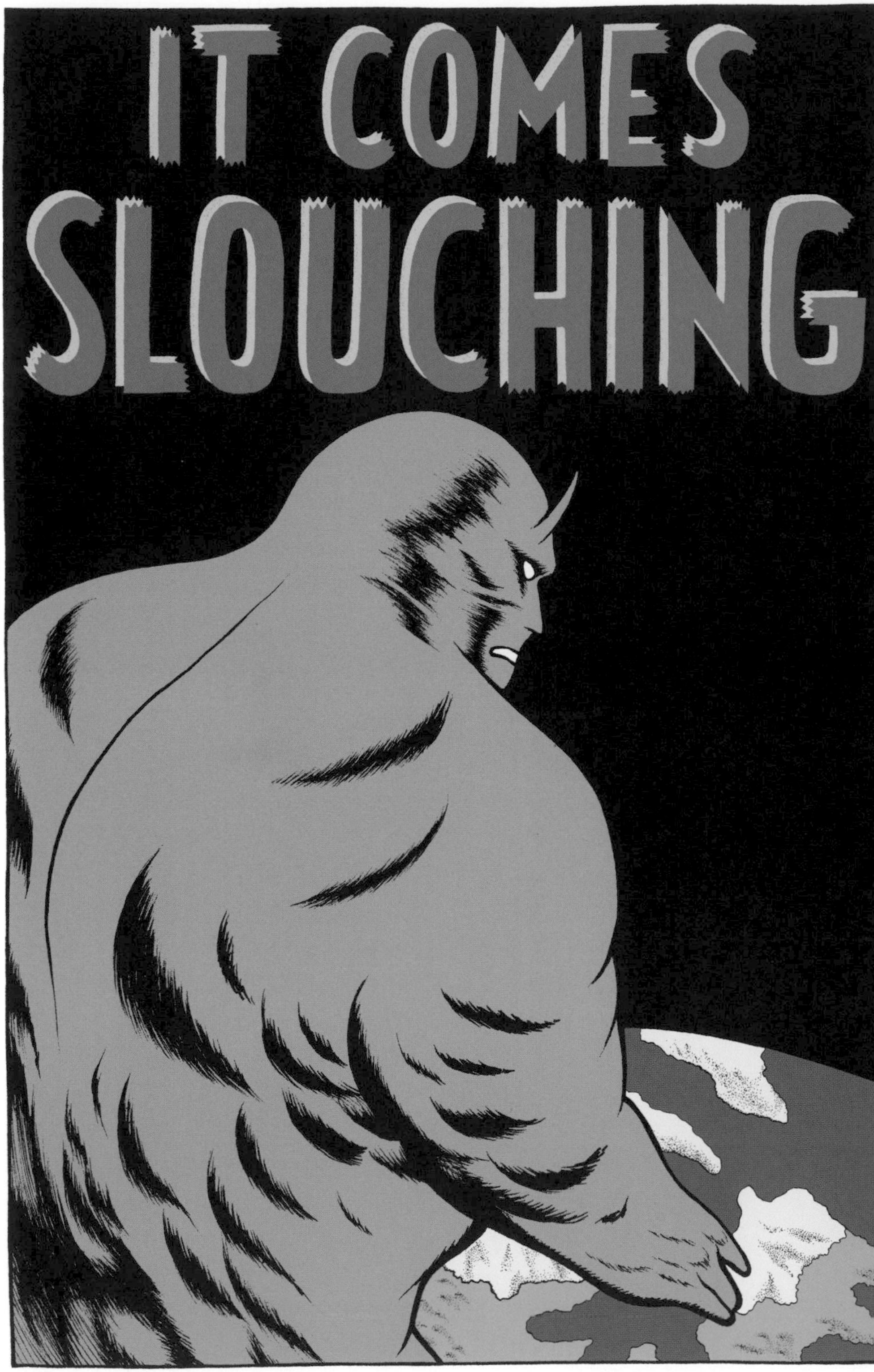
IT COMES
SLOUCHING

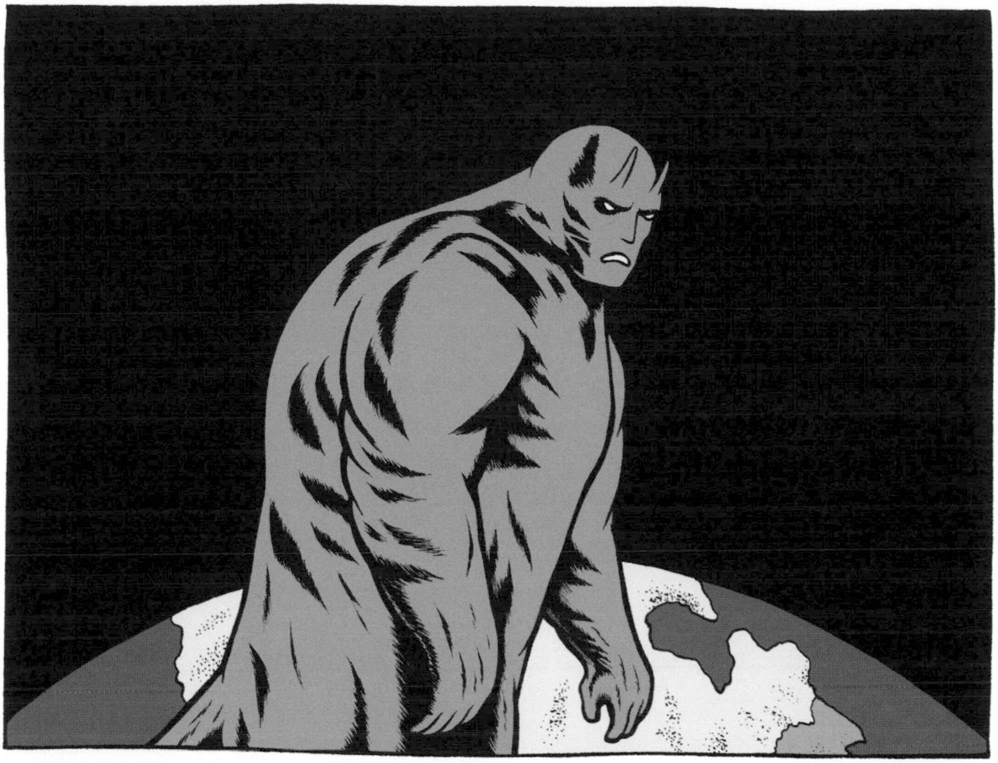

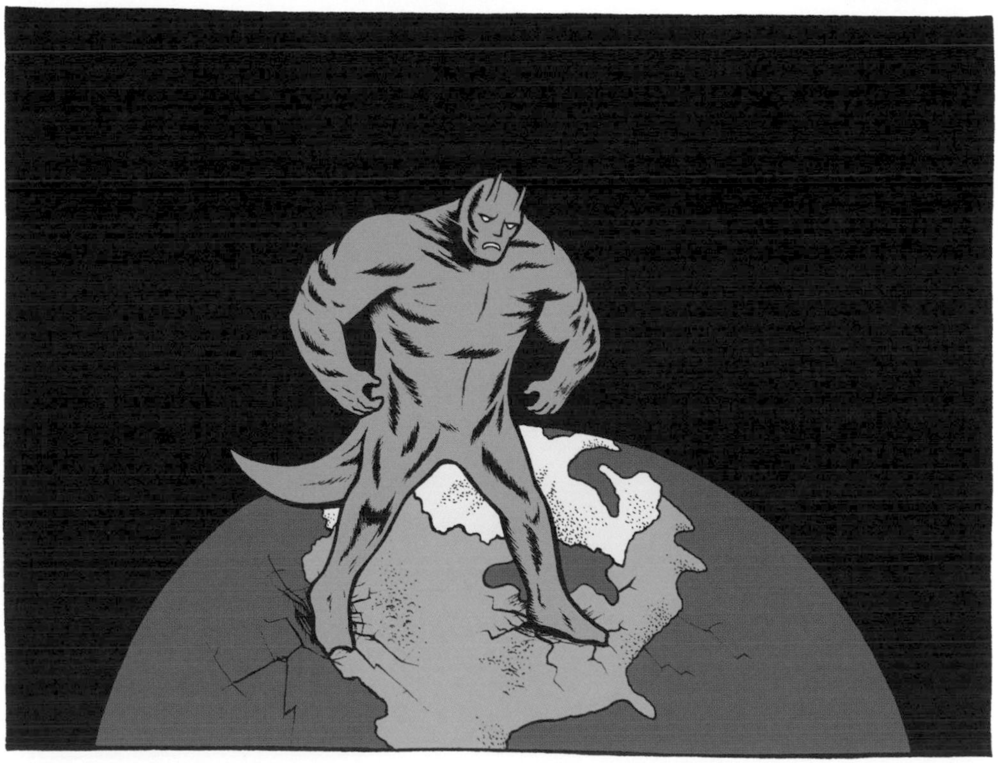

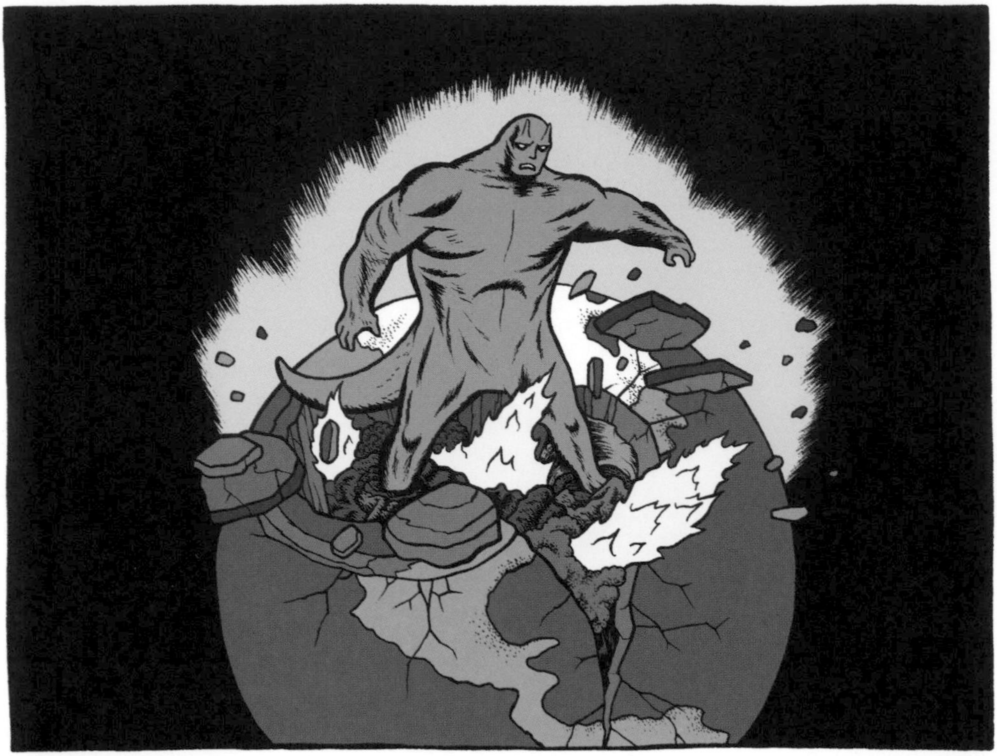

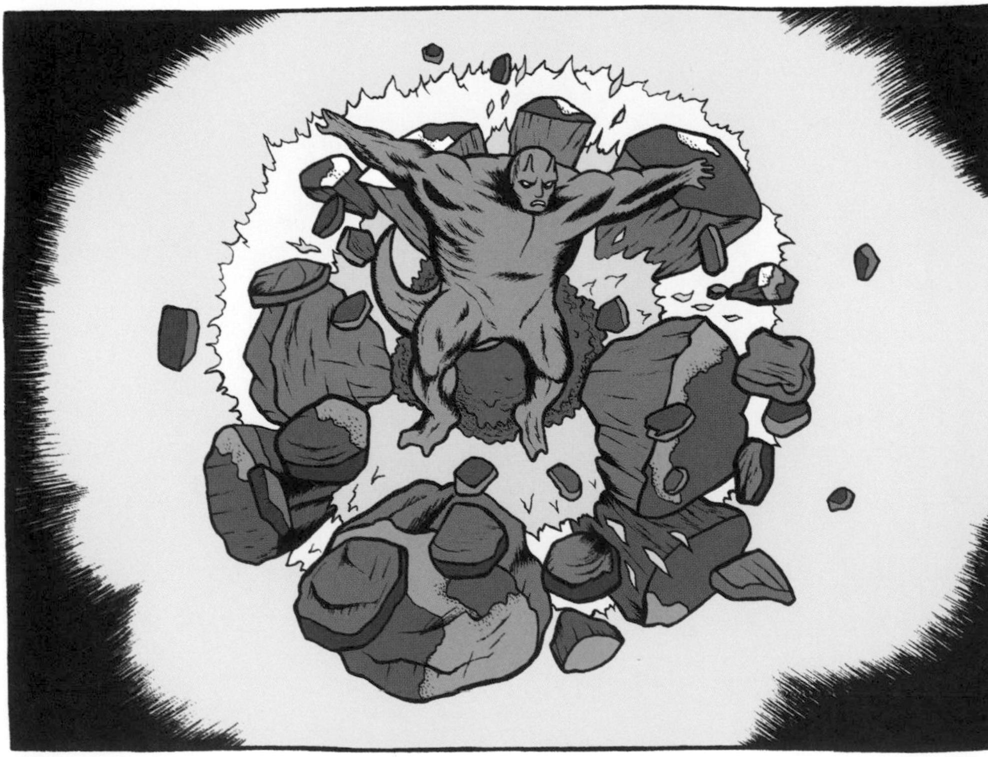

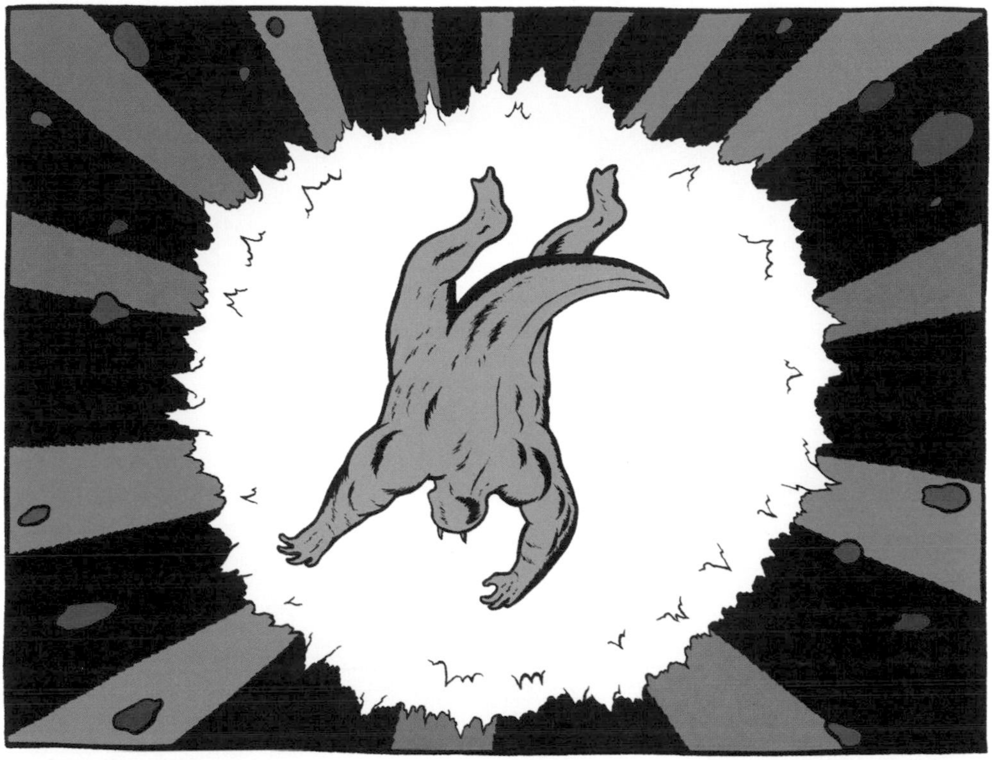

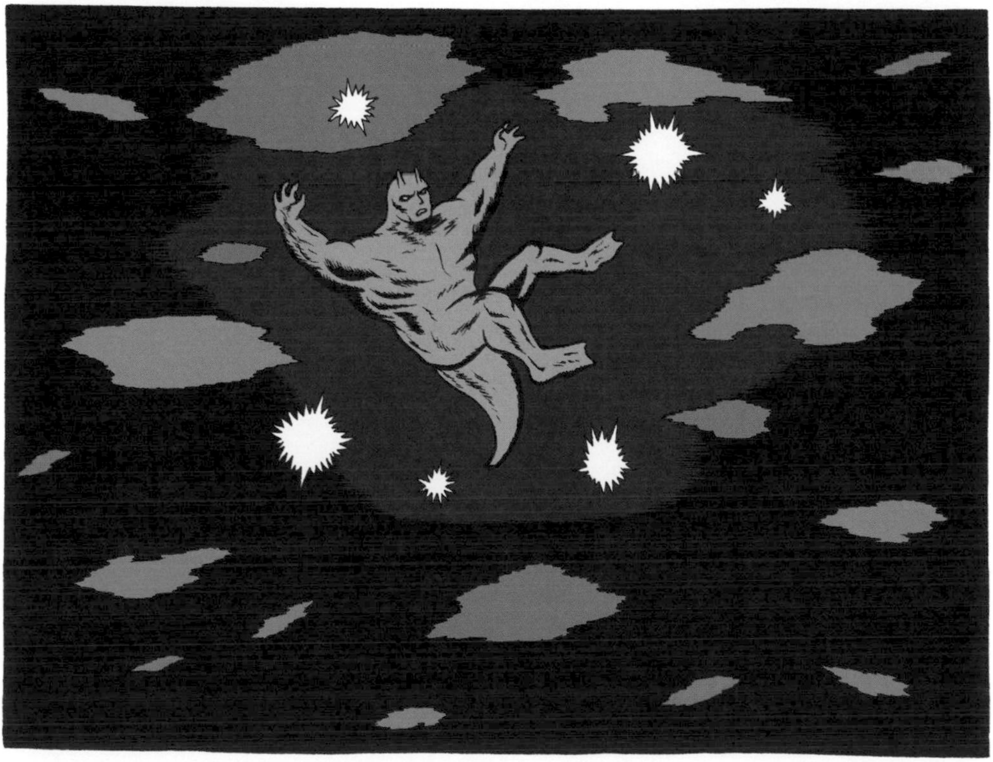

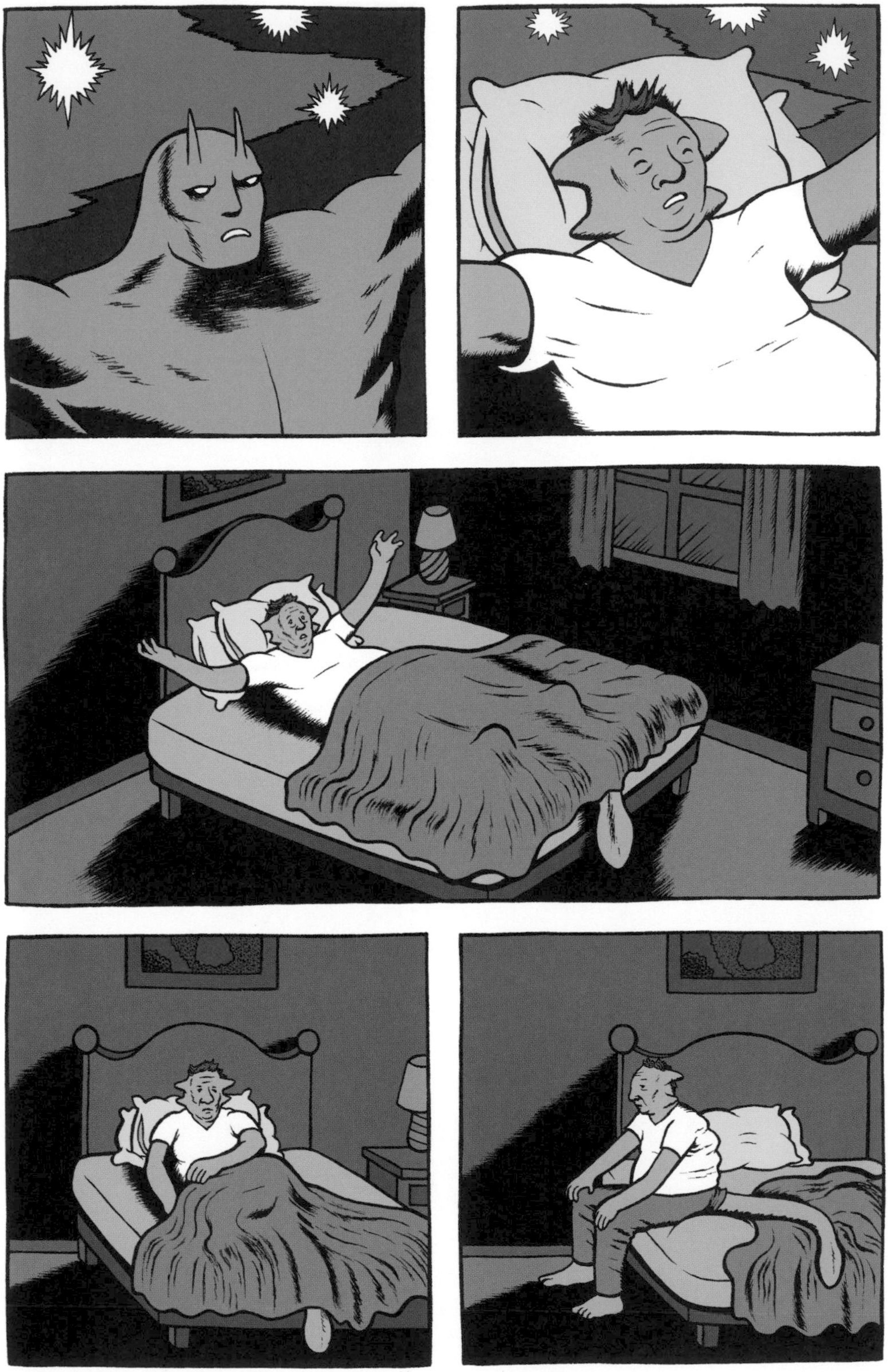

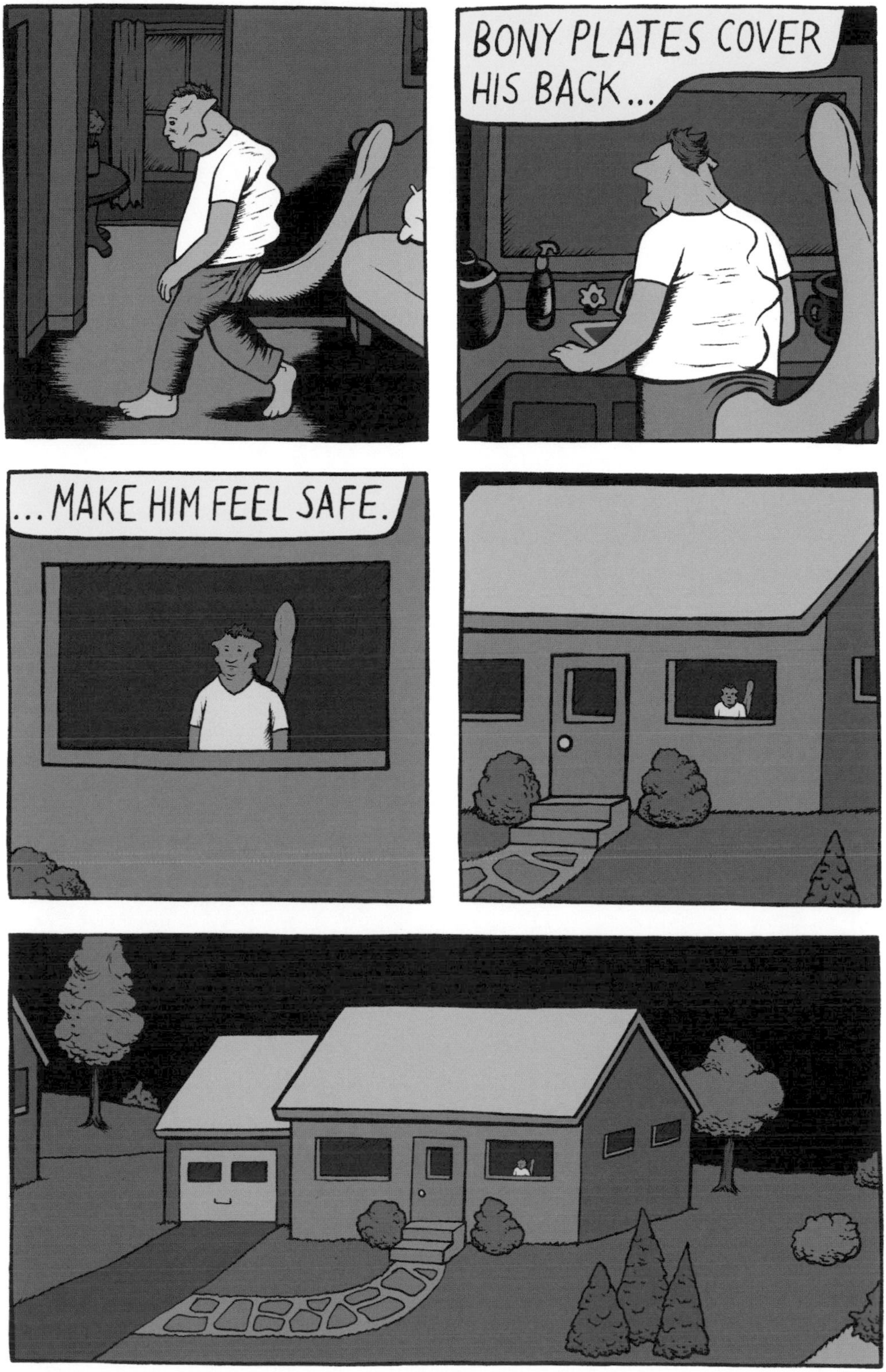
BONY PLATES COVER HIS BACK...
...MAKE HIM FEEL SAFE.

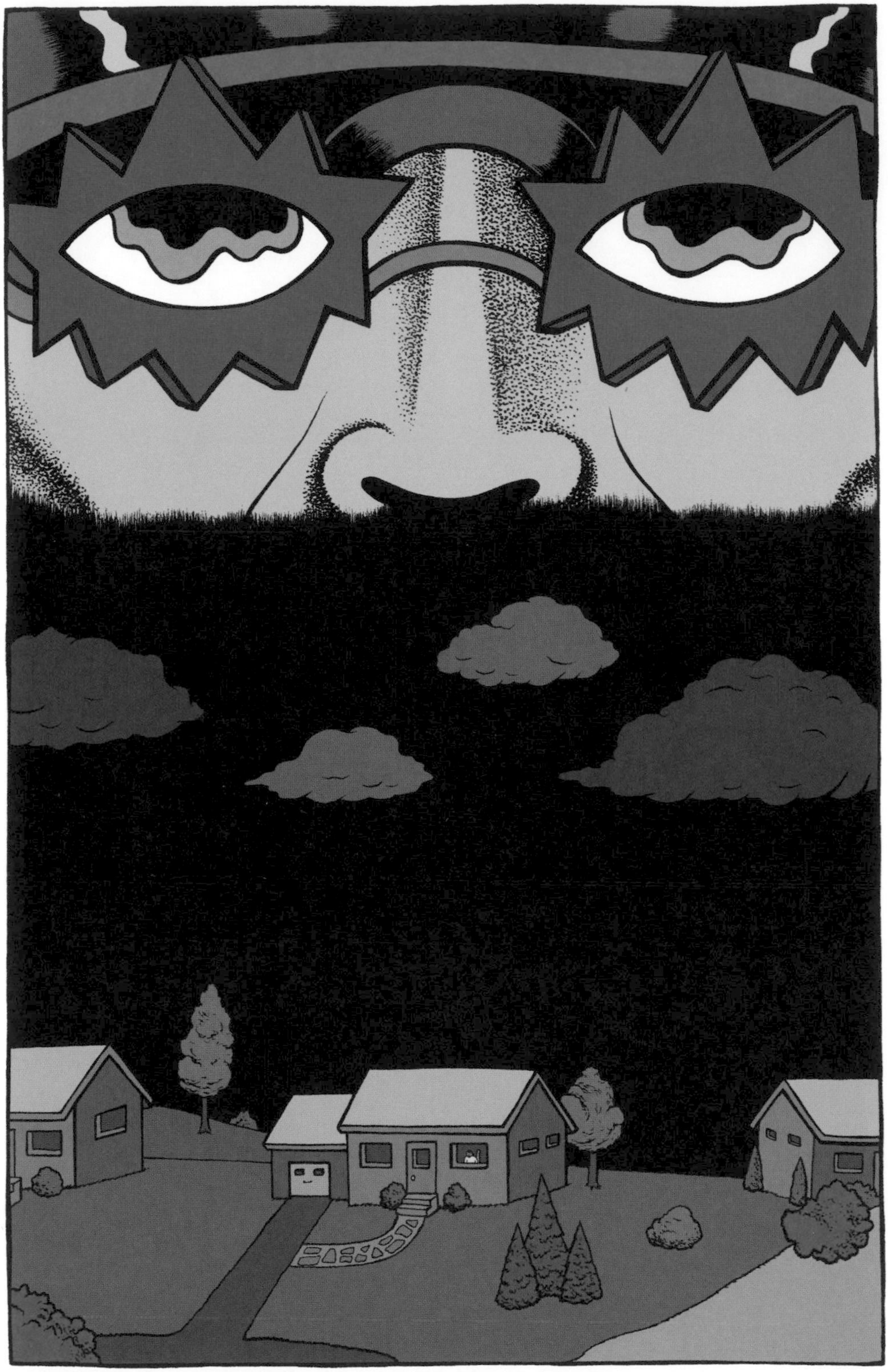

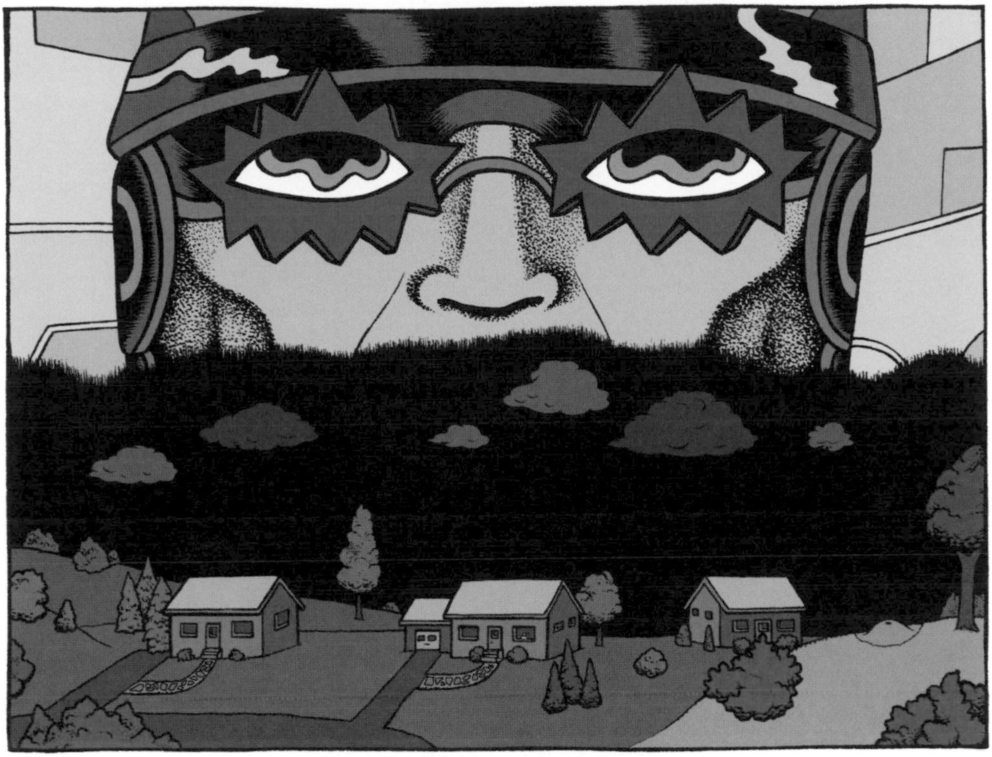

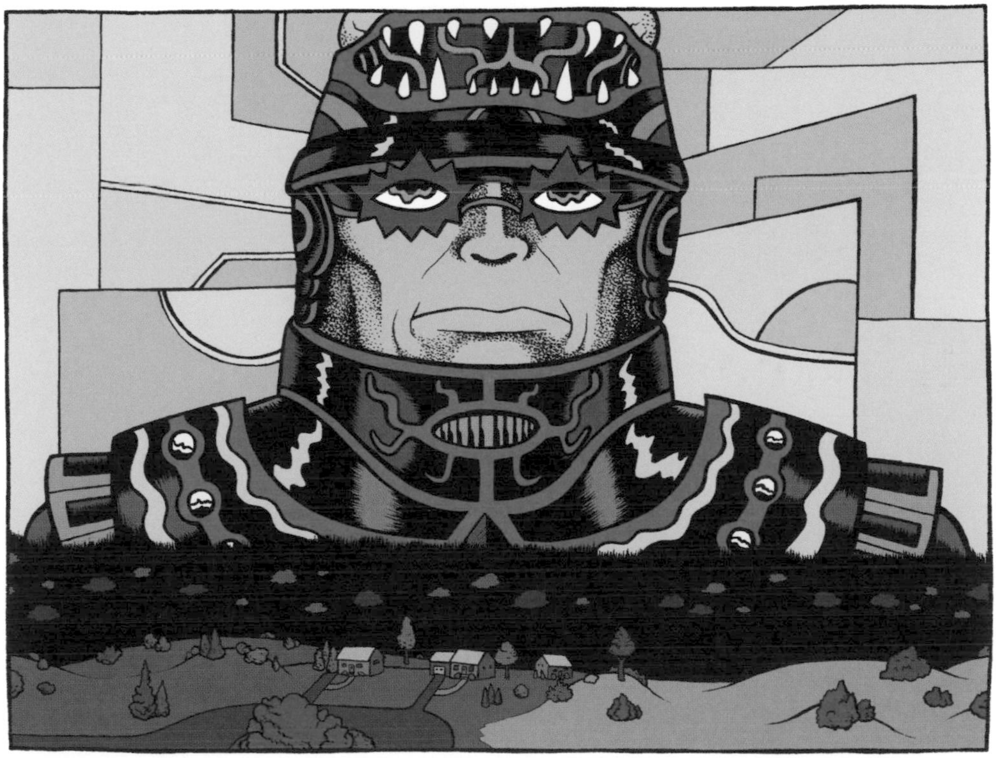

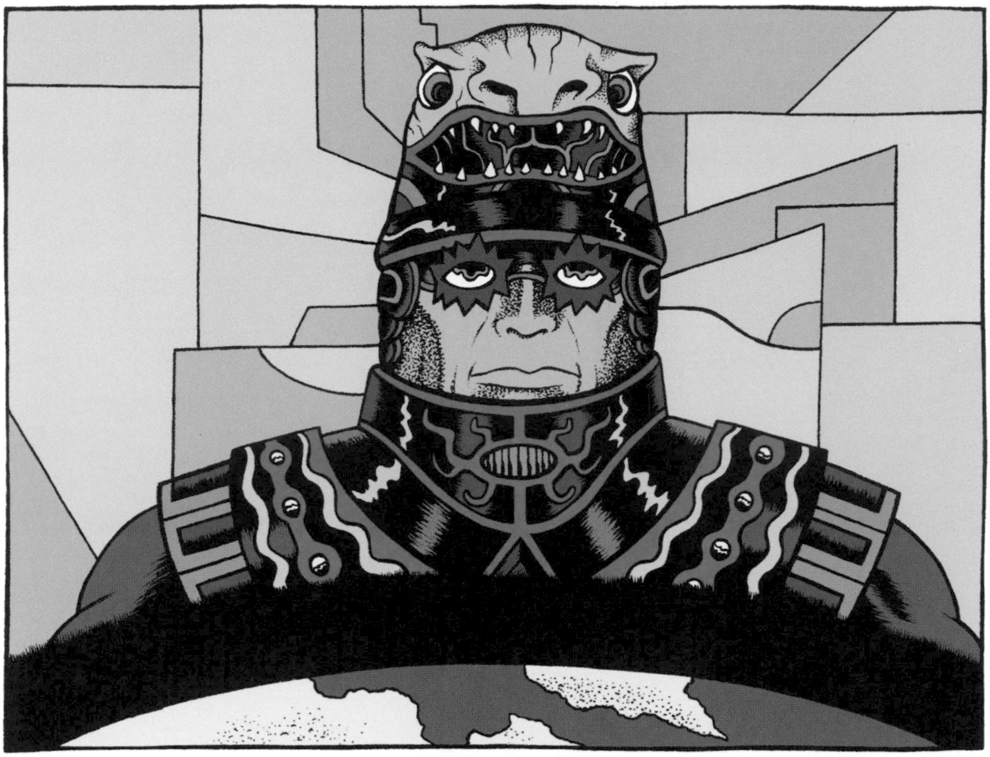

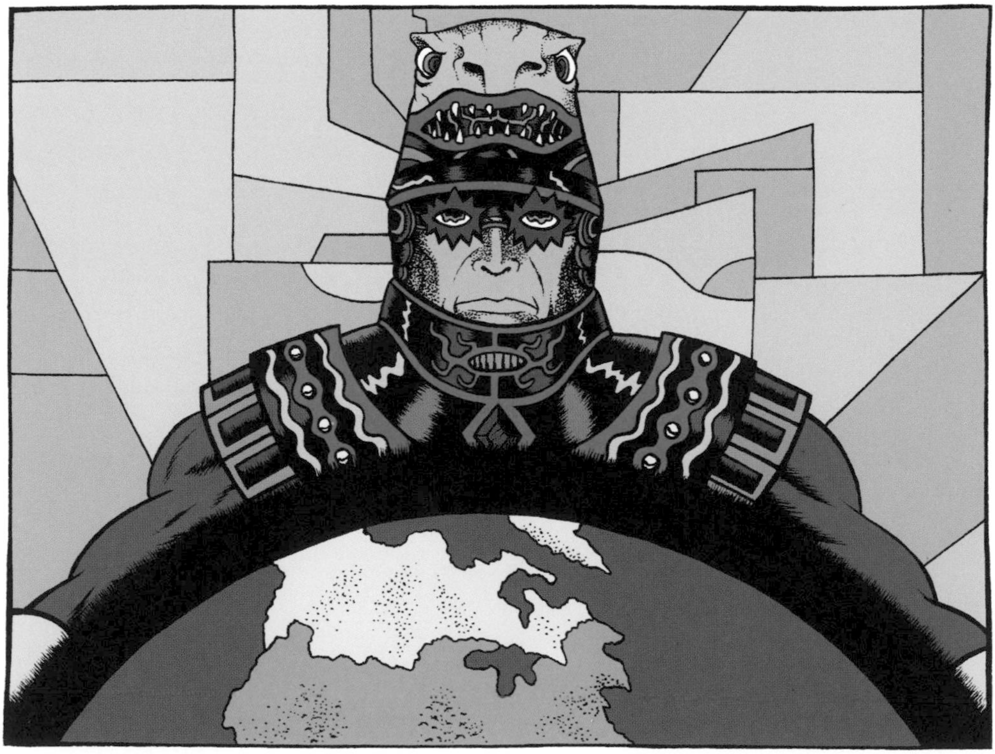

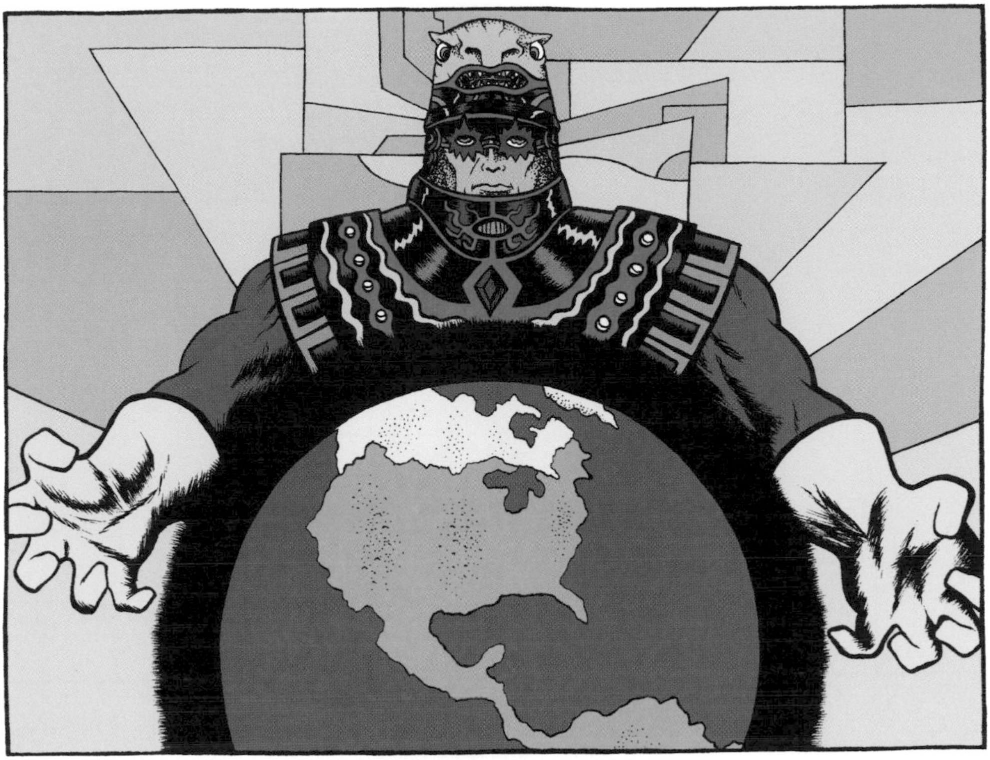

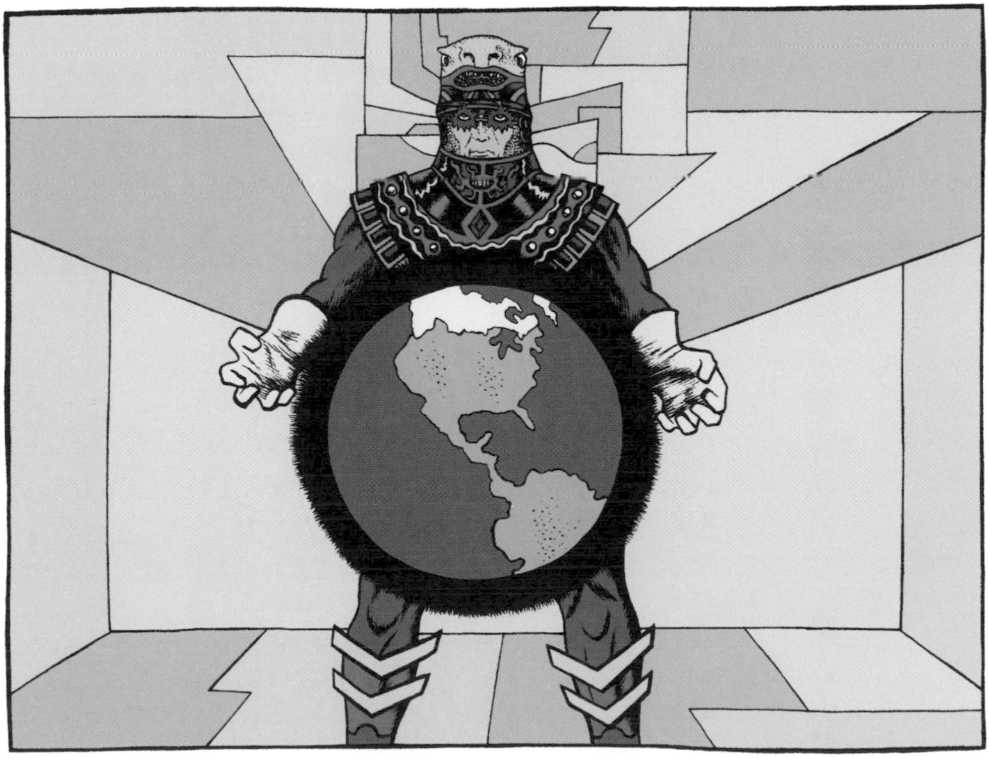

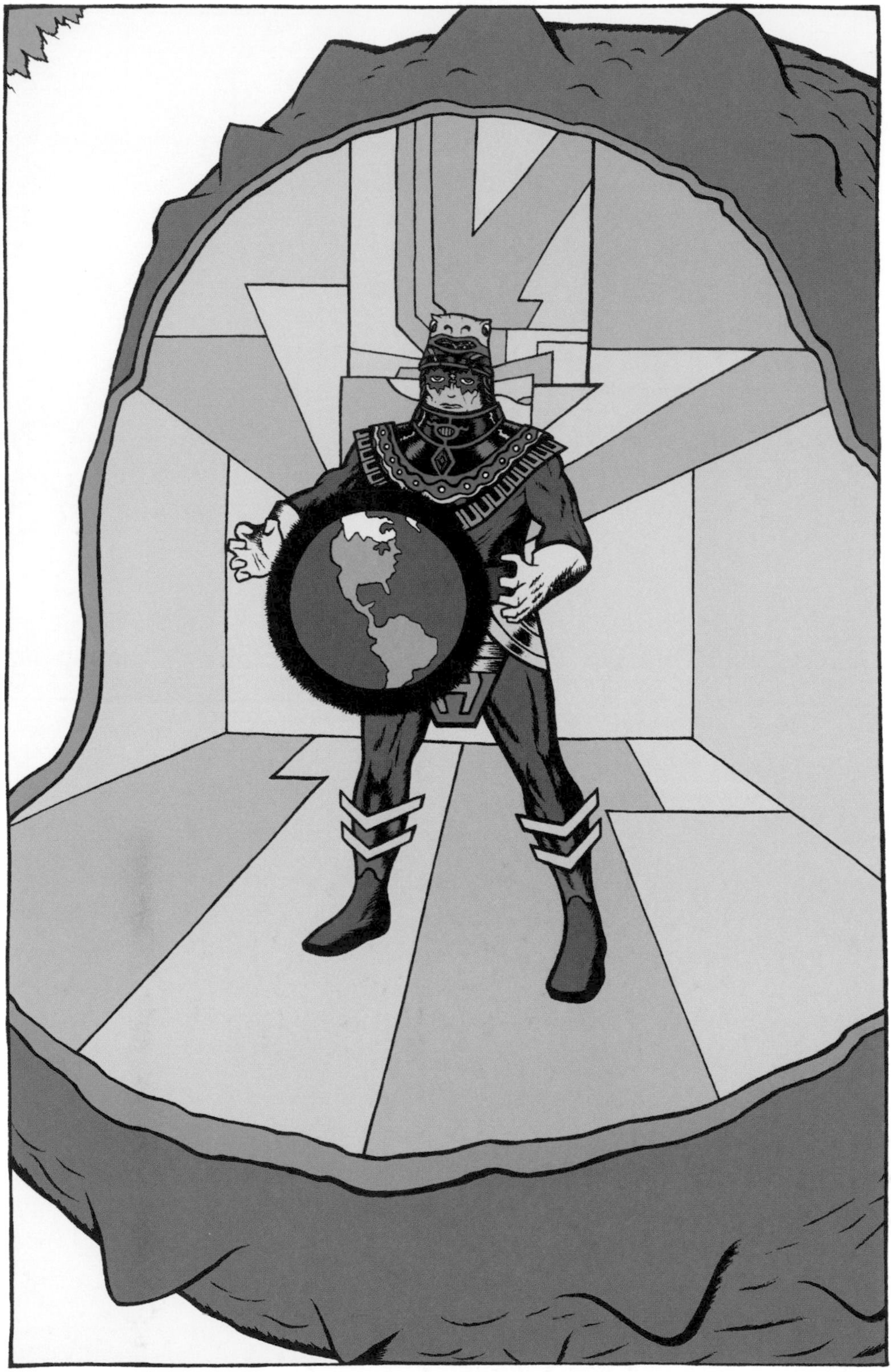

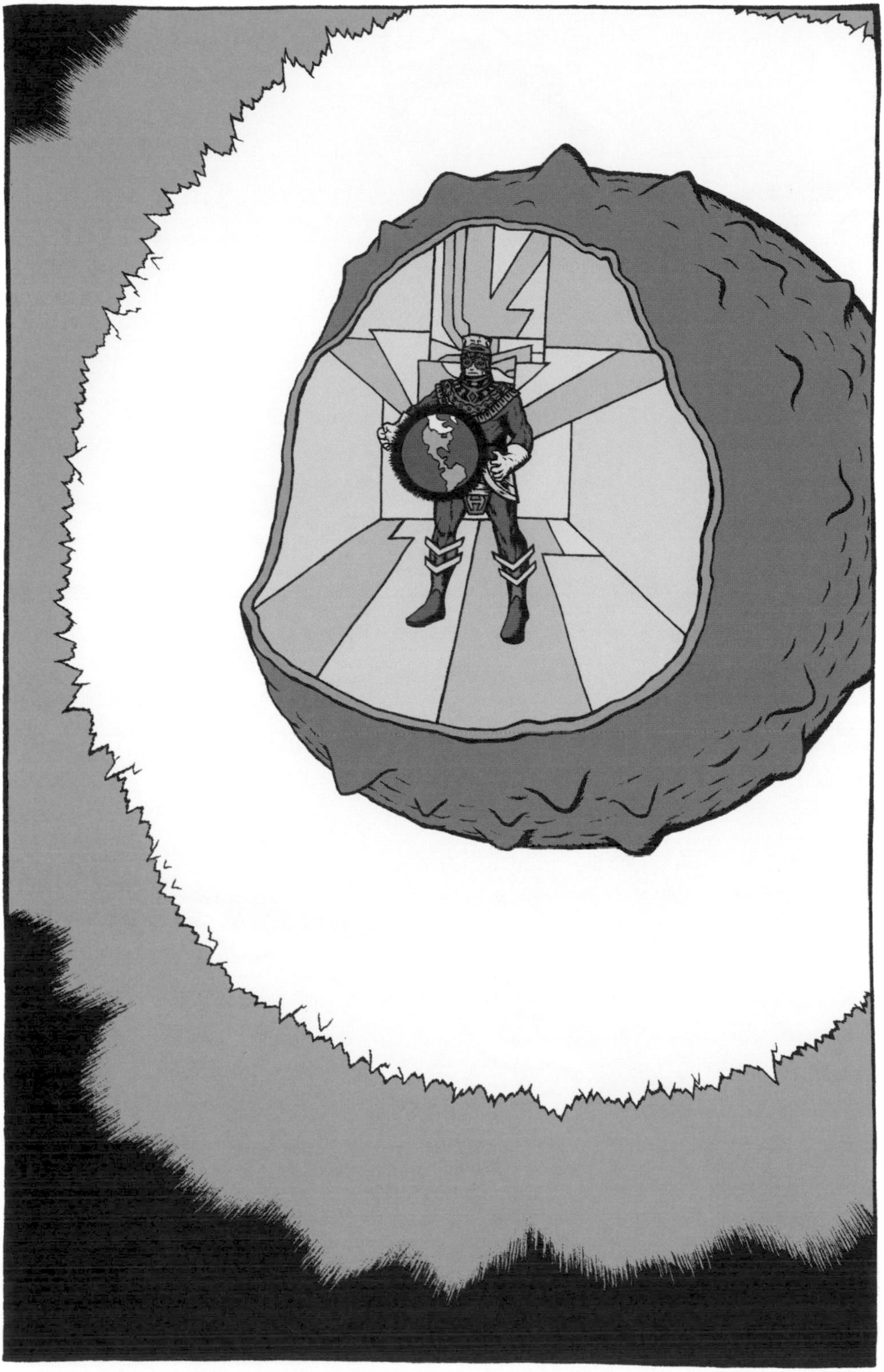

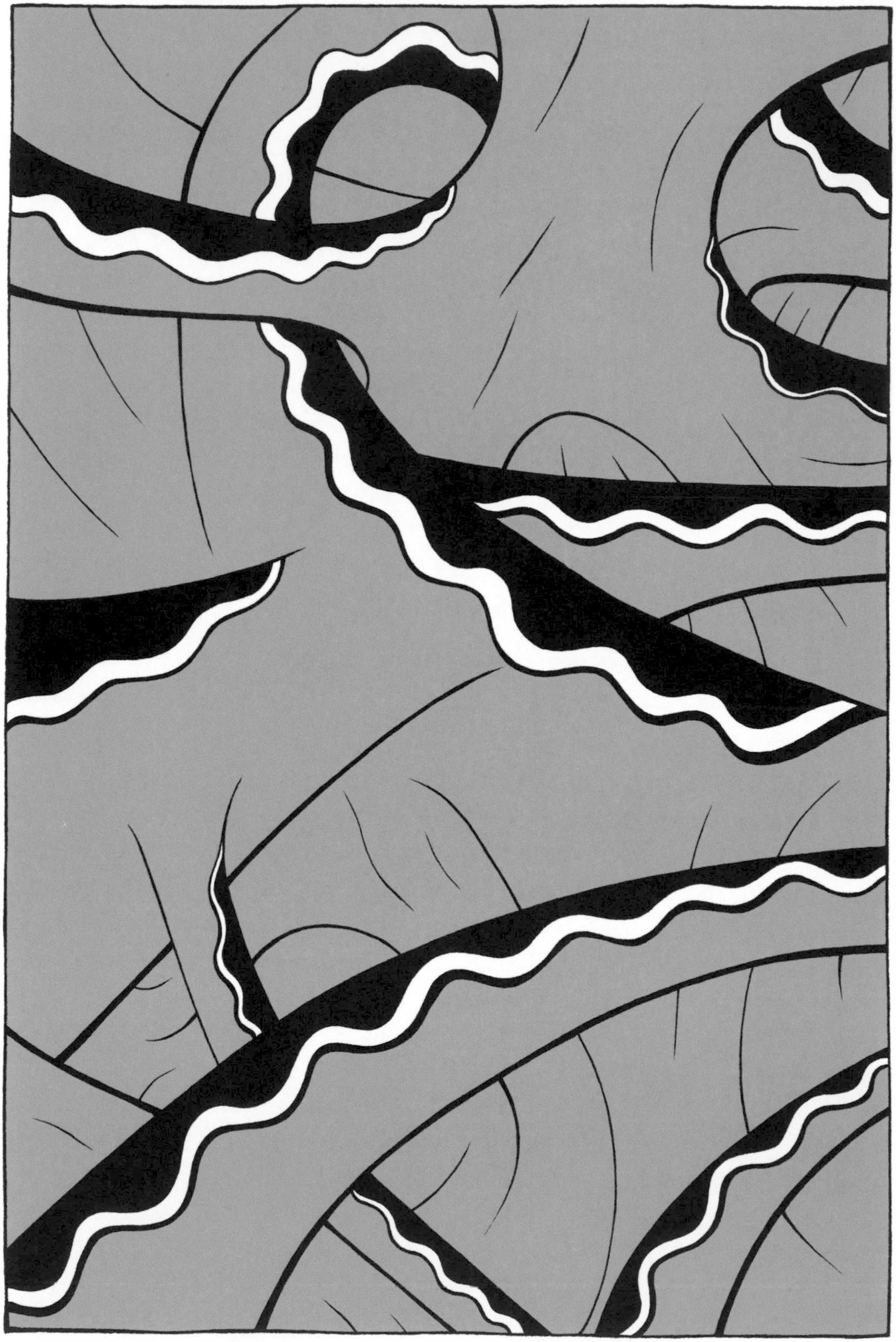

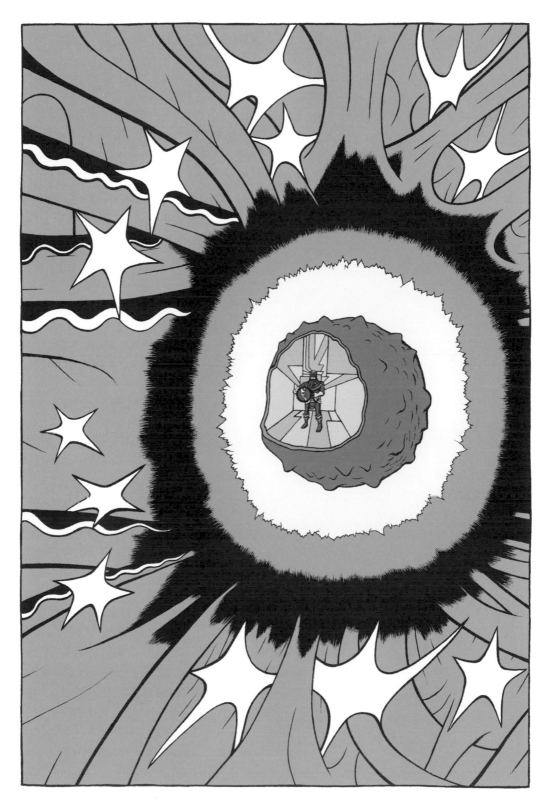

ERIC HAVEN'S COMICS HAVE APPEARED IN THE BELIEVER, LA WEEKLY, SF BAY GUARDIAN, AND MAD MAGAZINE. HE'S WRITTEN AND DRAWN TWO COLLECTIONS OF SHORT STORIES (COMPULSIVE COMICS AND UR) AND ONE PREVIOUS GRAPHIC NOVEL (VAGUE TALES). HE WAS AN EMMY-NOMINATED PRODUCER ON MYTHBUSTERS AND NOW WORKS IN TECH FOR X, A MYSTERIOUSLY SECRET COMPANY. HE LIVES IN SAN LEANDRO, CA, WITH HIS WIFE AND TWO CATS.

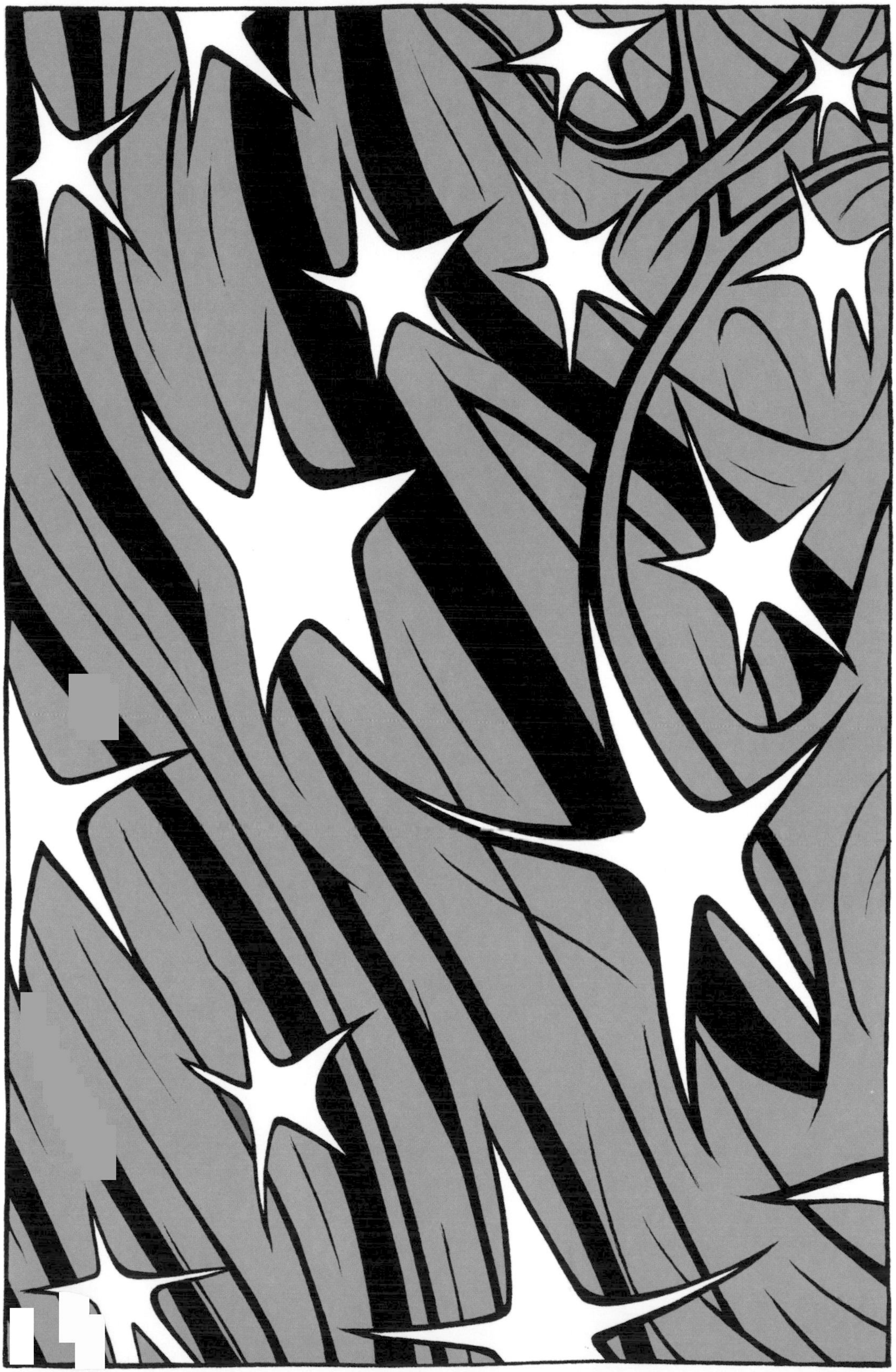

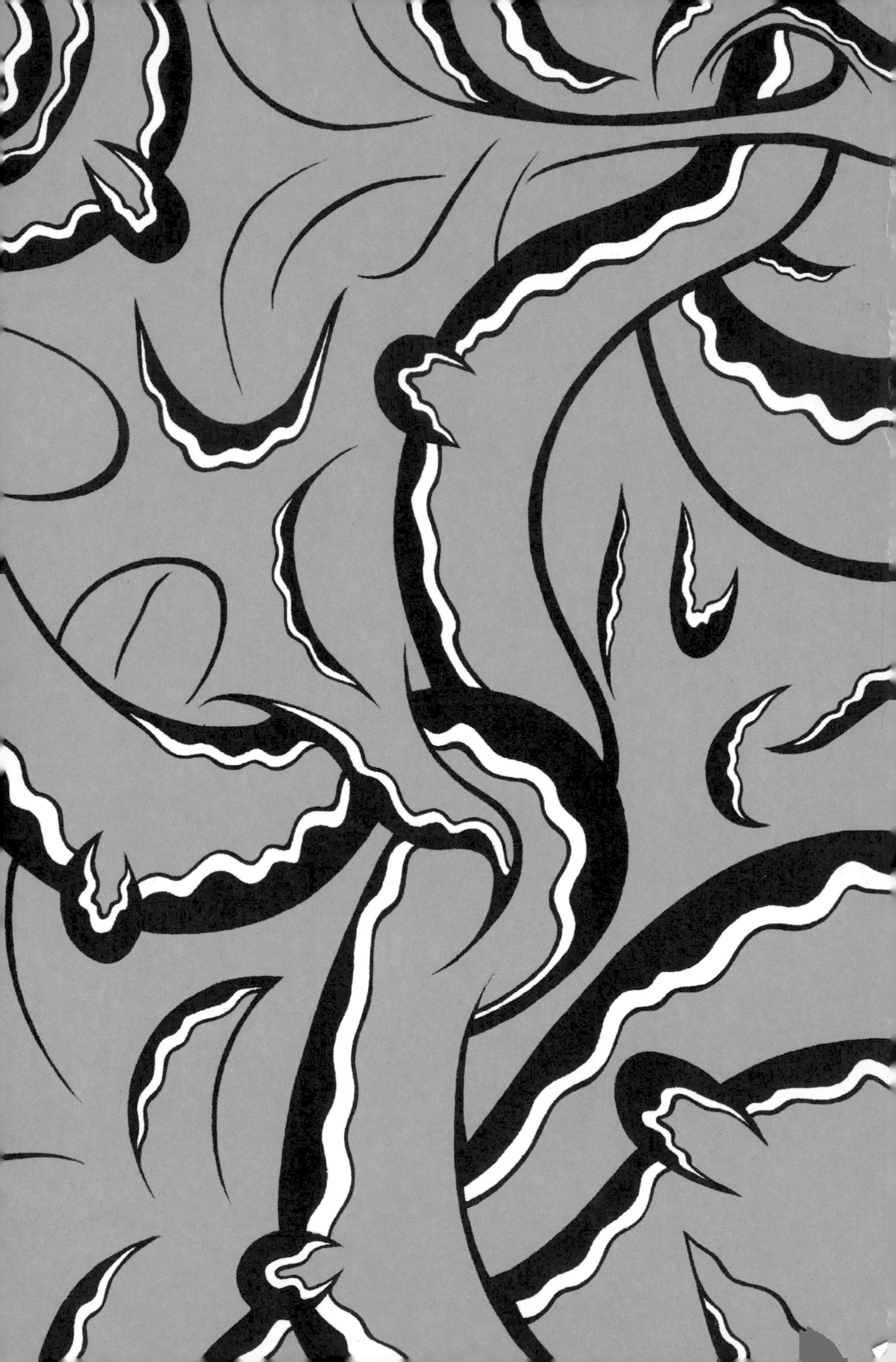